SMALL TOOLS HANDBOOK

SMALL TOOLS
Handbook

Peter Bishop

The Crowood Press

First published in 2000 by
The Crowood Press Ltd
Ramsbury, Marlborough
Wiltshire SN8 2HR

British Library Cataloguing-in-Publication Data
A catalogue record for this book is available from the British Library.

ISBN 1 86126 349 X

Line illustrations by Keith Field

All photographs by the author, unless credited otherwise

Designed and typeset by Focus Publishing, The Courtyard, 26 London Road, Sevenoaks, Kent TN13 1AP

Printed in Hong Kong by Paramount Printing Co., Ltd.

CONTENTS

ACKNOWLEDGEMENTS

An especially warm 'thank you' is owed to Peter Hunt from The Toolbank Group: without his skills of persuasion and help I would not have finished.

Words will not be enough to express the thanks due to those who have supported me in the preparation of this book: I list all and hope to miss none.

Atlas Copco Tools Ltd (AEG): Lesley Jewell;
Bahco Tools Ltd (formerly Sandvik Tools): Barry Ross;
Black & Decker: Colin Curtis;
BriMarc Associates: Geoff Brown and Charlotte O'Connell;
Crown Hand Tools Ltd: Charlotte Gandy;
DeWalt Industrial Power Tool Co. Ltd:
Mark Covill;
Hitachi Power Tools (UK) Ltd:
A.F.Tavener and Jacqueline Scott;
Microlene UK Ltd: Ron French;
Neil Tools Ltd (A Spear & Jackson Plc Group Co.): Drew Geldart and Sandra;
Paslode (an ITW Company): David Jordan;
Record Hand Tools: Peter Meorbeck;
Robert Bosch Ltd: John Roberts;
Screwfix Direct Ltd: Derek Skeavington and Cecile Byrne;
Senco Fastening Systems (UK) Ltd: Jim Fleming;
The Toolbank Group (Faithful Tools): Peter Hunt and Eddy;
also Julie McRobbie, Alan Wood and Mick Saunders.

INTRODUCTION

My father introduced me to tools. As a farmer he needed to be pretty handy, however he often had to 'make do', and because his tool kit and budget were limited, his tools therefore sometimes took a bit of punishment. In those days we certainly didn't have power tools – they were considered a luxury. As a boy I can recall watching, with my father, one of the first DIY shows on TV, with Barry Bucknel; we would both marvel at how easily things went together, though my father would explain this by saying 'Of course it's all pre-drilled and cut'. But then it would have been, because that's the right way to do it, even if we don't always choose that path. Our real problem was that we didn't have enough kit to do the job – and so I learnt to be adaptable.

Later, when I had started work at fifteen, Jack Morris the firm's carpenter introduced me to the 'Birmingham screwdriver' (more of that later). This was after an older lad advised me to put the hammer with a loose head into the brook to tighten it. That's OK, I hear you say – and so it would have been if someone hadn't replaced the handle with an old bit of pipe! Despite these asides, here I learnt quickly that good tools could help you do a better job faster.

As a trainee wood machinist I was poorly paid, and so I used to 'moonlight', making or working with wood. My toolbox started out with a few items my father gave me, and these were augmented by gifts or throw-outs. Occasionally tools were 'won' off a job, too – well, those careless enough to leave them lying around deserved to lose them! This in turn led me to find a way of making sure I didn't lose any of my own hard-won tools: I painted them bright red. I still have some tools and boxes today, well over thirty years later, clearly painted red or with some residue where hard work has worn it away.

A few of my first tools were acquired with cigarette coupons. In those days some cigarette companies courted smokers by offering coupons in each packet: these could be collected, and once a certain number had been amassed, exchanged for items out of a catalogue. My first set of bevel-edged chisels and my smoothing plane were acquired in this way – and I still have these, and use them today.

Tools, and especially woodworking tools, are fascinating, and I always hunt around in the antique shops to see what I can find, even though I don't often buy anything: although older tools are interesting, they are not of great practical value these days. Preparing for this book has given me the opportunity to handle a large number of new tools: much to my wife Norma's consternation, our house has at times looked like a storage depot! During these months, boxes of various sizes and shapes arrived containing a wide range of hand and powered tools, many of which feature in these pages. I was meant to send them all back, though needless to say some were retained – on favourable terms, of course! – to augment my toolbox.

Over the years I have surrounded myself with many different tools and gadgets to make life easier – when I could afford them. In this, several overriding principles apply, including the following: first, if a certain tool can be afforded and will save time, then buy it; second, if the job in hand will stand the purchase, then buy it; and third, always buy the best that is available, or at least the best that you can afford. Long, useful life is important. And although there are some exceptions today – for instance, a saw with hardened teeth – basically the message is the same as it always has been: look after your kit, keep tools clean, sharp and tidy, and they'll look after you. Remember the old adage, 'a good craftsman never blames his tools'.

I hope readers will find this book interesting, and above all useful; and I trust that you will spend many happy hours in your workshop creating things with this wonderful material: wood.

FIRST IMPRESSIONS

Workers of wood have a variety of identities. To earn a living I undertake various tasks: for example, in the context of this book I make furniture and write about it – although I have no formal qualifications as a 'cabinet maker' and therefore do not claim to be one. It does also slightly annoy me when I am called a 'carpenter', especially when it is obvious that those concerned simply don't know the difference between, say, joinery and bodging. One of the official training courses available in my time – and one which, I might add, I managed to pass with credit! – was 'The Advanced Craft Certificate in Machine Woodworking: Joinery, City and Guilds of London Institute' – whatever that might mean: even I don't altogether know or understand what exactly it implies!

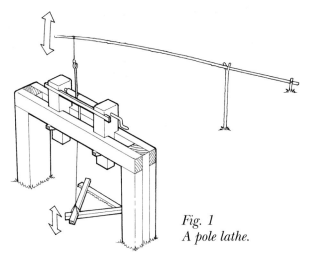

Fig. 1
A *pole lathe*.

WOODWORKERS CATEGORIZED

In my opinion the following classifications pertaining to a career in woodworking may be explained as follows:

THE BODGER

Bodgers were a dying breed but are now enjoying something of a revival. Originally based in coppice woods, they were employed to turn, or bodge, legs and other components for chair makers. They used a simple 'pole lathe' which was easily transported from one work site to another.

THE CABINET MAKER

These exceptional craftspeople are concerned with furniture making or 'cabinet work'. In most instances each piece or project is a wholly independent item not directly joined to anything else. It is also considered that cabinet making refers to good quality work rather than something thrown together with screws and dowels!

THE CARPENTER

Carpentry applies to the structural part of woodworking in buildings, and any heavy wooden engineering applications. A carpenter is therefore trained to prepare constructional and structural woodwork such as a roof. In the trade this is called the 'first fix'.

THE DIY-er

This term describes a new 'breed' of do-it-yourself merchants, their ability ranging from the incompetent to the exceptional. They will tackle all aspects of household-related building, including repairs and maintenance, and they do not confine themselves to woodwork.

THE FURNITURE MAKER

Similar to the cabinet maker, though perhaps not as highly qualified; the furniture maker will probably also be less experienced as regards time spent in the business.

THE JOINER

The joiner's craft is preparing the wood finishings for buildings. These are not structural: carpenters do that. They are, however, generally more decorative, and include windows, doors and stairs. This end of the trade is called 'second fix'.

THE PATTERN MAKER

This craft entails the preparation of wooden moulds and models from which metal castings can be made; it is another which is becoming obsolete.

THE WOODWORKER

This is the 'catch-all' name that embraces us all. Calling yourself a woodworker avoids any rigid categorization, especially if you don't measure up to, or dislike being allocated to, any of the above!

A whole host of other wood-related trades used to have, or still do have, their own description. Yet in today's training courses, carpentry and joinery seem to be put together, and cabinet making is dealt with as something different altogether. In fact most 'woodworkers' will have to have skills in a wide range of applications from turning to veneering. Basically, if you like working with wood then continue to enjoy it, and don't worry about what people might call you. Wood is such a warm and forgiving material that it should be appreciated at every opportunity.

UPDATING YOUR TOOLS

Some purists will argue that the best methods of construction are obtained using traditional tools, a contention with which I agree to a certain extent. I would make a comparison with the modern-day maths teaching practice of using a calculator, namely that this is perfectly acceptable provided that in the first instance every pupil knows how the sums work. The same applies to woodworking tools, in that even if your workshop is fully mechanized you still need to understand the basic principles. Once these are clearly established, however, there is no reason why, for example, the smoothing plane may not be dropped for the portable hand planer, or the larger stand-

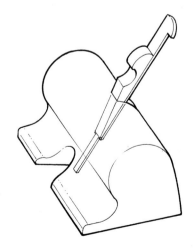

Fig. 2 An 'old woman's tooth'.

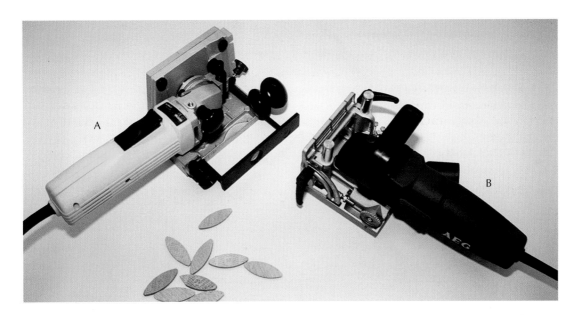

Fig. 3 Biscuit jointers: a: vertical; b: horizontal.

alone planer. Can you imagine our forefathers sweating and straining today with an 'Old Woman's Tooth' (Fig. 2), the precursor to the modern-day router? I am quite sure they wouldn't, unless it suited them to do so.

I am not advocating that we abandon or ignore altogether our older woodworking tools; but when a job can be done as well as, or better, and more quickly by using powered tools, then we should consider using them. As I have already mentioned, I still have tools that I acquired over thirty years ago, most of which are used fairly regularly; however, since then I have updated my kit as time and money have allowed – although I have to admit that I have often stubbornly refused to try out certain tools or practices which at the time were new or innovative. For instance, when I first started writing for the popular woodworking press, 'biscuit' jointers (Fig. 3) were increasingly being used. I persisted in rubbing joints or using loose tongues because I could not see the advantage of these machines – until,

inevitably, I was lent one for a sponsored article and all at once I realized why

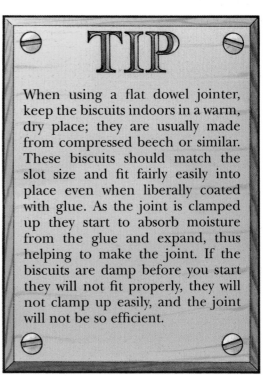

TIP

When using a flat dowel jointer, keep the biscuits indoors in a warm, dry place; they are usually made from compressed beech or similar. These biscuits should match the slot size and fit fairly easily into place even when liberally coated with glue. As the joint is clamped up they start to absorb moisture from the glue and expand, thus helping to make the joint. If the biscuits are damp before you start they will not fit properly, they will not clamp up easily, and the joint will not be so efficient.

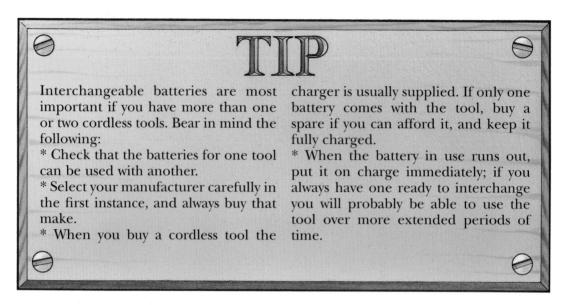

TIP

Interchangeable batteries are most important if you have more than one or two cordless tools. Bear in mind the following:
* Check that the batteries for one tool can be used with another.
* Select your manufacturer carefully in the first instance, and always buy that make.
* When you buy a cordless tool the charger is usually supplied. If only one battery comes with the tool, buy a spare if you can afford it, and keep it fully charged.
* When the battery in use runs out, put it on charge immediately; if you always have one ready to interchange you will probably be able to use the tool over more extended periods of time.

everyone else was so much in favour of them. Providing they are used correctly they make an excellent joint, and for most of my 'top' works I will now use one of these flat dowel jointers – their correct name – instead of my old techniques.

CORDLESS TOOLS

In recent years manufacturers have designed and enhanced some magnificent cordless tools. Initially battery life was limited, and this disadvantage, together with inadequate power delivery and the high cost of the tools, did not make cordless kit very attractive. Today, however, a whole range of alternative cordless tools is available for a wide variety of jobs. Technology has moved on from the simple screwdrivers that ran out of power too soon, to a range of standard and percussion drills, saws and other goodies. For the really heavy-duty stuff they are not yet fully developed, but it will not be long before they are.

One of the neatest sets of cordless kit I have seen comes from Black and Decker (Fig. 4), and although no heavyweight, it has been specifically designed to be versatile. For instance all the batteries are interchangeable, and the drill head on one of the tools may be easily swopped to sander, and to jigsaw. This useful range, although not robust enough for site work, could form the cable-free basis for any workshop. I would guess that, as time goes on, more and more power tools will become cordless and more sophisticated.

GAS-OPERATED TOOLS

Also cordless, there are some very exciting gas-operated tools coming onto the general market at the present time, and as technology develops these tools are becoming increasingly cost-effective. For example, the Paslode framing nailer (Fig. 5) has a gas-powered linear combustion engine fired by battery-powered electronic ignition; it is most suitable for those jobs where repetitive nailing is required, and because it weighs only 3kg or so it is easy to carry around – on a roof, for instance. An immensely powerful tool, it can fire up to 1,000 nails per hour continuously. The size of nails for this particular nailer range from 50mm up to 90mm long and can be driven right into

Fig. 4 Part of a multi-purpose tool range with some interchangeable heads and universal batteries.

Fig. 5 Alternative hammers: a: gas-operated nailer; b: air-operated nailer.

Fig. 6 A selection of lightweight and heavyweight nails for use in air- and gas-operated nailers.

most woods (Fig. 6). The magazine is angled back so that the operator is able to reach into awkward corners, and the depth of drive can be set to suit particular needs. This is a heavy-duty piece of kit. It tends to leave a slight surface mark after the nail has been fired and is therefore best used for 'first fix' applications.

The same firm supplies a finishing nailer. This tool fires smaller pins, from 19mm through to 64mm (Fig. 7), without leaving a surface mark: because the pins are only 16 gauge they hardly show at all when embedded; also the depth of drive can be adjusted to finish flush or below surface for filling. It has a soft tip to avoid marking at the end on the nailing nose. The manufacturer claims that nearly 2,000 fasteners can be used for each fuel cell, and the battery needs charging after every 4,000. Because of its lighter touch

the finishing nailer is ideal for 'second fixing' – skirtings, architraves, beadings, panels and so on.

AIR-OPERATED TOOLS

If becoming cordless is not crucial to you, then consideration should be given to air-operated tools; indeed a lot of commercial workshops have been using air power for some time. In fact the kit itself has never been too expensive, but one of the larger costs has always been the air compressor. Today, however, you can get a complete package very reasonably because compressor sizes and costs have reduced. Senco produce the 'Accuset' range (Fig. 5) and manufacture a number of tools targeted at the smaller woodworking operation: light and versatile, the large range covers nailers through to staplers –

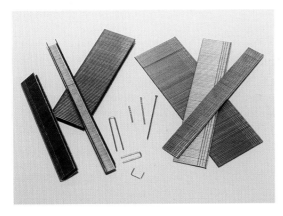

Fig. 7 A selection of staples and pins for air- and gas-operated fixing tools.

depending upon the tools, pins and nails from 12mm to 65mm can be used, and staples from 12mm to 40mm (Fig. 7). With the right connections, additional tools such as screwdrivers and wrenches can be added. The versatility, lightness and power delivery of these tools make them ideal for any modern workshop.

Gas- and air-operated tools have been popular in the USA for some time and are becoming more common daily. They offer good value for money, especially if there is a large amount of fixing to be done. However, although the price of the tools has come down, watch how much you are expected to pay for the ancillary bits and pieces: it is worth shopping around to find out where these can be purchased most cost effectively. Also try to establish if a manufacturer's nails or staples are interchangeable: if they are, one might work out to be cheaper than another. There will almost certainly be further developments in this sector of tool design in the near future, and as technological advances are made, such tools will become more readily available to the general woodworker. At the moment I don't have any in my workshop, but I am quite sure it won't be long before I do!

IN SUMMARY

When you are thinking of buying any particular tools, first establish what you want them for initially, then consider if they are likely to satisfy a future need. For instance a picture framer would probably be best served by buying a guillotine (Fig. 8): provided he looked after it and maintained it regularly, it would almost certainly be well worth the investment. It is also important to think of cost. Occasional use warrants a cheaper tool than one in constant use – though having said that, if you can afford it, always trade up because good tools last longer. And of course all tools will benefit from regular maintenance, so don't neglect them.

Fig. 8 A manually operated guillotine machine cutting mitres. (Record Hand Tools)

— 2 —

SETTING UP
THE WORKPLACE

THE BUILDING

Workshop buildings will come in a variety of shapes and sizes. Each of us will probably have some idea of an ideal set-up, though it is debatable whether we will ever achieve it!

The first workshop that I can remember clearly was in my father's garage, many years ago. I had moved back in with my parents, and in fact stayed with them for a couple of years, and I needed to supplement my poorly paid rep.'s income. Space was a bit tight in the garage, so we built a narrow workbench under a window on one side – every time I needed to do anything we had to run the car outside. In winter it was very cold, so most of my work was scheduled for warmer weather. For convenience I made some racks for my meagre collection of tools: things that were used often were kept close at hand, either behind the bench or to one side; clamps and other bigger bits of kit hung down the side of one garage wall. After each successful commission I ploughed some of the proceeds back into

Fig. 9 Old and new 'workmates'.

tools. Early on I saved up and bought my first workmate, and this soon paid for itself many times over – in fact I still have this trusty bit of kit. The new ones are even more impressive (Fig. 9).

After this interlude at home I moved back to the main yard operation of the business, and became involved in management. I had little or no time for bench-work: living on my own, I changed address probably every six or twelve months, and my kit was packed away and little used. However, eventually I settled down and married. Our first home was a restoration project, a country cottage with an old barn attached – and as far as I was concerned, the latter is what sold it. It was all in need of thorough repair, so we started with the workshop – naturally! This time I set out the benches around the walls and positioned the windows to suit. I had a lot more kit by then, including a bandsaw, a lathe and a universal machine. We concreted the floor, although I very quickly discovered that concrete was quite tough on the feet if I stood at the bench all day; the solution was to roll out some old lengths of carpet, as these helped provide a cushion. All the tools were racked or clipped so that they were easily to hand.

I bought my first vacuum at this time. Friends and colleagues were always surprised to see how clean and tidy I kept the workshop, but I was taught that a tidy workplace produced tidy work. So I always put my tools away in the same place; this way nothing gets lost, and you can soon tell if something is missing. I also try – though don't always succeed – to put tools away in good condition, in other words sharp and clean. There is nothing more frustrating than starting a job and finding that all the kit needs sorting out first.

My occupancy of this workshop lasted as long as it took to do the house up and then sell it on. Our next property was a small farm with a few acres and lots of

buildings – and once again it was the potential for workshop space that sold the place for me. This was of course the first project completed: located in a large steel portal-frame barn, I covered in the sides with weather-boarding, and waterproofed the roof; I had some large metal-framed windows fitted right down the southern aspect to give plenty of light; and I made sure the floor was raised and boarded to avoid the previous problems with concrete. I had a woodburning stove, fitted benches and lots of storage space – and indeed, at trying times my wife would occasionally suggest I move in there!

This workshop became my base for the next eight years, a long stay for us. I extended the range of powered, stand-alone machines, which ultimately included a different bandsaw, the old lathe, a crosscut saw, a ripsaw, an over-and-under planer and a pillar drill. These were augmented with a widening range of small powered and hand tools. It was here that I seriously returned to bench-work, once I had decided to quit the commercial rat race. I also started writing at that time, and recall one editor of a popular magazine waxing lyrical about my workshop; I don't think he had ever seen one so well organized and tidy! My daughter Daisy joined our family whilst we were here, and this brought other problems with it: as she became more mobile I had to start shutting, then locking, the workshop door.

Time moves on, circumstances change, and we decided to sell. This time we moved in to rented accommodation, a house belonging to an old farming friend; he also had a building where I could temporarily house my workshop – in one end of a sheep shed! In fact I was there for just over a year, and produced some lovely work and had the benefit of company whilst I did so. By this time I had learnt that for me, at least, it was better to make

TIP

If you are working with powered tools in a workshop make sure you are not disturbed: if you are concentrating hard, the last thing you need is an unexpected interruption. My family know not to do this in case I might cut something off, and make a noise when approaching so that I know they are coming. Set up a bell system and lock the door. But – and this is a big but – make sure that someone knows where you are, and how long you expect to be working at this particular job, and make sure they can get in if anything goes wrong. It's also a good idea to put a sign on the door to keep children out. Finally, isolate all electrical equipment before you leave. This is all common sense really, but it is important to be safety conscious to avoid any chance of damage to you, or to anyone else.

the benches transportable. Until then I had always built them in for stability, but the problem was that, when we moved, either the benches had to stay, or inevitably they were damaged when we took them out. This time, therefore, I constructed a long, flat-topped bench with two vices – and this is still in use today. In addition I had a large, square bench that could be used to lay things out on. All my tools had to be locked away each night for security, as the building was open. Fortunately I had acquired a shipping container somewhere, and this held our surplus furniture and household goods in one end and all my tools in the other.

The workshop was not ideal, but I coped. One of the main problems in winter was the amount of dust created by the sheep when they were housed in the barn; for instance, if I was sealing or polishing something, it had to dry off pretty quickly because left overnight a layer of dust would appear all over it. However, eventually we found another property to buy.

Our current premises occupy what was originally an old village shop and Post Office. Closed down through lack of support and cash flow problems, the premises had been vacant for a couple of years. I now have two separate buildings: one houses my stock of timber and the fuming chamber; the other has two working areas – and once again I am fortunate in having plenty of space. The strategy adopted for the previous workshop has worked, the mobile benches just slotting into place (Fig. 10), and I have developed this further so that all the tool racks can now be taken down and re-erected elsewhere. I have also extended my range of old kitchen cupboards to house all the ancillary bits and pieces.

IN SUMMARY

To summarize, it really does not matter where or how big your workshop building is, because you will always grow into the space available. There are, however, some basic requirements that you should try to consider, and some to avoid if possible – unfortunately we can't all afford purpose-built premises.

* Try to keep the workshop dry and warm: if you are making furniture for use in today's modern houses it will need to be

Fig. 10 Part of the author's workshop at the time of writing.

worked in a damp-free environment to avoid shrinkage later.

* Try to arrange plenty of ventilation for hot summers – if you don't, your working conditions might become pretty uncomfortable.

* Low metal roofs are to be avoided if at all possible: they are very hot in the summer and extremely cold in the winter, and they also create problems with condensation.

* If you can afford it, heat your workshop: this might be a woodburning stove or a portable gas heater, though a purpose-built workshop could be linked to a central heating system. Insulate the walls and ceiling if at all possible.

* As I discovered to my discomfort, concrete floors are hard and cold. You do need a firm level surface, however, so if you are stuck with concrete, cover it with old carpets, or fit a suitable board face over the top.

* Lighting is important. My current workshop has two north-facing windows and is rather dark; this means I rely heavily on strip lights. Ideally try and have southwest- or southeast-facing windows. Direct sunlight is not recommended, but you will manage if it's all you have. If you have to use strip lights, make sure they all work, and keep them clean; take advice from your electrical supplier on the best type to use.

* Fit as many power points as possible – double sockets are best. Fit them yourself if you have the knowledge, but be sure they are safe; personally I prefer to employ a qualified electrician. The more sockets you have, the less chance there is of tripping over a trailing lead. You can also leave tools plugged in ready for action!

* If you have a big enough budget, consider fitting an extraction and/or filtration unit, as fine dust can be extremely detrimental to your health.

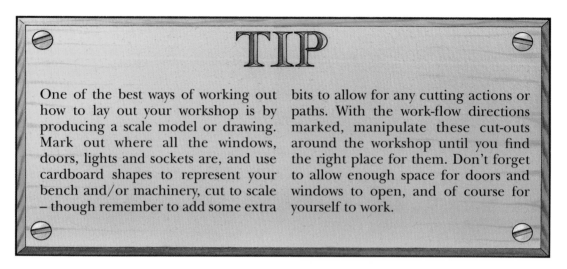

One of the best ways of working out how to lay out your workshop is by producing a scale model or drawing. Mark out where all the windows, doors, lights and sockets are, and use cardboard shapes to represent your bench and/or machinery, cut to scale – though remember to add some extra bits to allow for any cutting actions or paths. With the work-flow directions marked, manipulate these cut-outs around the workshop until you find the right place for them. Don't forget to allow enough space for doors and windows to open, and of course for yourself to work.

(These units are covered in more detail in Chapter 9.)

THE WORKBENCH

A workbench generally becomes the focal point of the workshop, and careful consideration should be given to its size and shape before you buy one or spend time making one. It may be that initially, like me, all you can afford is a few flat boards fitted to a frame, but don't let this worry you, because some beautiful work has been created from such humble sources. The bench should always be as solidly built as possible to provide a firm working surface. A joiner's bench generally has a flat surface, and this is the type I prefer to work on.

Try and think through what you are going to be making: for instance, large joinery items such as stairs, doors and windows will need plenty of work surface; whereas for furniture or cabinet making, less will suffice. The height of the bench is crucial, too: unless you are exceptionally tall or short, a comfortable working height will be something between 800mm to 900mm. Basically, you should be able to

Fig. 11 Two different ways to fix simple vices. (Record Hand Tools)

stand comfortably, working at the vice, for longish periods without ending up with backache. Also, to control your tools correctly you will need to be above them, working down and away – holding a hand plane at about waist level will give a fair indication of the best height; another way is to measure your inside leg, like a tailor, and add 50mm to it. Both methods will give you nearly the same result.

It helps if you can put tools away as you finish with them, and to this end you can make or buy a bench with a tool well: this is a recess towards the back of the bench into which tools can be dropped and left

Fig. 12 A range of bench vices. Note the 'dogs' on the two in the foreground. (Record Hand Tools)

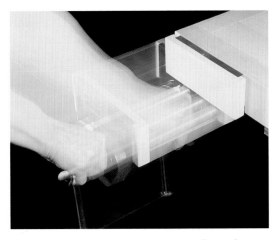

Fig. 13 Auto-slide vice in action. (Record Hand Tools)

as the work carries on. However, make sure the well is deep enough to accommodate the tools that are likely to be left in it – it is ultimately frustrating if you move a workpiece around the bench

and ride over the top of a tool in the well! To my mind the best option is to have a tool rack at the back of the bench, and put the kit away.

VICES AND STOPS

A vice is an essential on any bench, and there are many types. There are simple bolt-on or clamp-on vices (Fig. 11), having just a basic function of winding in and out to hold the workpiece in place, and there are more sophisticated vices that might incorporate a 'dog', an adjustable vertical stop, against which the workpiece can be placed (Fig. 12). Some of these vices also have an automatic release mechanism so you don't have to wind them in and out on the thread all the time (Fig. 13). Whichever type of vice you choose, be sure to fit it with timber protectors or pads over the metal faces; generally these can just be screwed into place through the body of the vice. Some ready-made benches will have an end vice fitted (Fig. 14); using dogs, these can be very useful for holding awkward-shaped items. And if you want to build your own, the mechanisms are readily available for purchase. Once again, what you need will

Fig. 14 An example of an end vice and adjustable bench dogs. (BriMarc Associates)

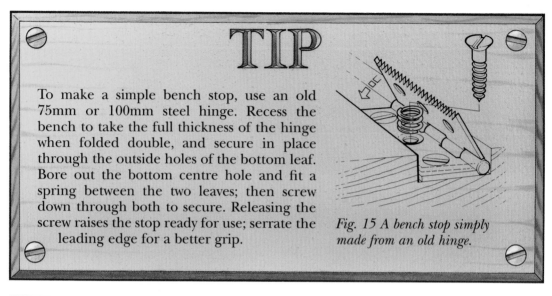

TIP

To make a simple bench stop, use an old 75mm or 100mm steel hinge. Recess the bench to take the full thickness of the hinge when folded double, and secure in place through the outside holes of the bottom leaf. Bore out the bottom centre hole and fit a spring between the two leaves; then screw down through both to secure. Releasing the screw raises the stop ready for use; serrate the leading edge for a better grip.

Fig. 15 A bench stop simply made from an old hinge.

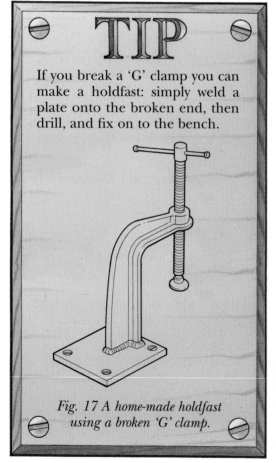

TIP

If you break a 'G' clamp you can make a holdfast: simply weld a plate onto the broken end, then drill, and fix on to the bench.

Fig. 17 A home-made holdfast using a broken 'G' clamp.

depend upon the type of work you will be carrying out – and also the depth of your pocket! Adjustable integral bench stops are useful, as work can be pushed against these and held fast; some can be located at the end of the bench, and others at strategic points along it.

Another useful accessory that can easily be fitted to the workbench is a holdfast (Fig. 16). These enable you to hold different shapes and sizes firmly in place while you work on them.

Fig. 16 Two sizes of adjustable bench 'holdfasts'. (Record Hand Tools)

HOOKS

Bench hooks are a very useful addition to any basic workshop kit (see Figs 19a and 18a/b), and may be simply constructed from odds and ends, or bought in ready-made. They can fit over the edge of your bench, into the vice or the jaws of a workmate. They are excellent for holding small to medium-sized pieces of wood whilst cutting across the grain.

CUTTING MITRES

Cutting mitres is made easier if you have a mitre block. These can be simple, one-sided affairs, or they are of a box construction to give better saw stability (Fig. 19b/c); these boxes are available ready cut, although for site work it is a simple exercise to make your own. If more sophisticated guides are required, then think about a metal one that will clamp your workpiece in place (Fig. 19d). And for really accurate mitre sawing, choose a specialist mitre saw system (Fig. 19e): this type of set-up allows you to swing the saw guides from side to side into pre-set locations for accuracy of cut every time. They can also be set at right-angles, thus potentially doing away with the bench hook, and at various other

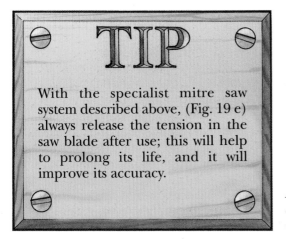

TIP

With the specialist mitre saw system described above, (Fig. 19 e) always release the tension in the saw blade after use; this will help to prolong its life, and it will improve its accuracy.

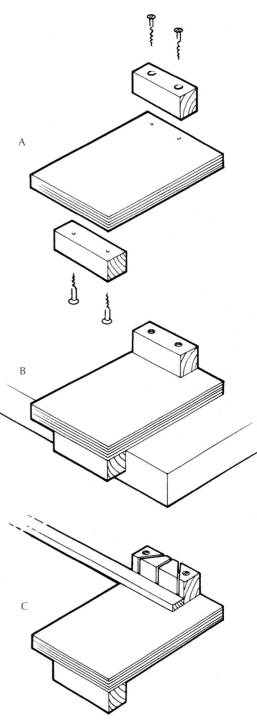

A

B

C

Fig. 18 a and b: make a simple bench hook; c: enhance the versatility of your bench hook, incorporated guide cuts.

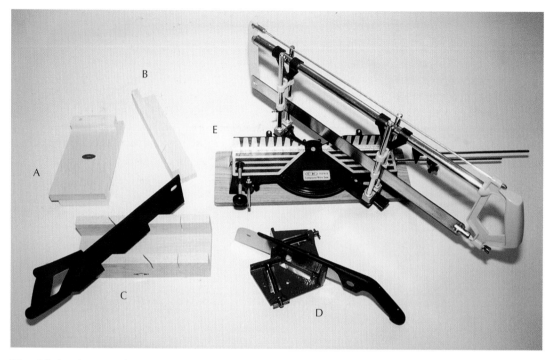

Fig. 19 A selection of sawing aids: a: simple bench hook; b: single-sided mitre and right-angle guide; c: double-sided mitre block; d: metal saw guide and holding device; e: sophisticated compound mitre saw and guide arrangement.

angles as well; the one illustrated can cut 'compound' mitres – that is, mitres on two planes.

There are other more simple, but probably less accurate, ways of making guides to cut mitres. The simple bench hook can be marked and cut out for this (Fig. 18c); alternatively a guide with two legs can be constructed for use in a vice or workmate (Fig. 20d). For gripping thin pieces of wood whilst you work on them you might make a slight modification to your bench hook (Fig. 20a). A similar device can be made with a couple of pivoting jaws fitted to a board or directly to your workbench (Fig. 20b). For repetitive length-cutting by hand, set up a simple bench hook with an adjustable stop (Fig. 20c).

All the workbench aids are useful and time-saving, and their versatility and design is only limited by your own imagination and need.

CARE AND MAINTENANCE

Look after your workbench: keep it flat, clean and tidy. Any oil or paint spills will mark your work if left in place. Also, clean off dried glue: many times I have seen work ruined because a scratch has appeared on a finished surface. It does no harm to sand off and clean down the top regularly, and a light waxing afterwards will help with the tidying-up process. If the top has become damaged, consider re-skinning it with an additional layer of good quality ply. Cupboards and drawers below will be extremely useful; however, make sure they are a good fit because dust will inevitably get in.

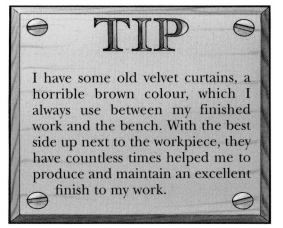

TIP

I have some old velvet curtains, a horrible brown colour, which I always use between my finished work and the bench. With the best side up next to the workpiece, they have countless times helped me to produce and maintain an excellent finish to my work.

WORK BOXES, BAGS AND STORAGE

If you can afford it and have the space, fit another bench, slightly lower, on which you can assemble components. Always maximize the space available by storing things below your benches: in addition to clearing some of the clutter away from the top surface, it will help the benches to be more stable. Limited space calls for innovation, yet some of the best ideas are very simple. A mobile storage unit and

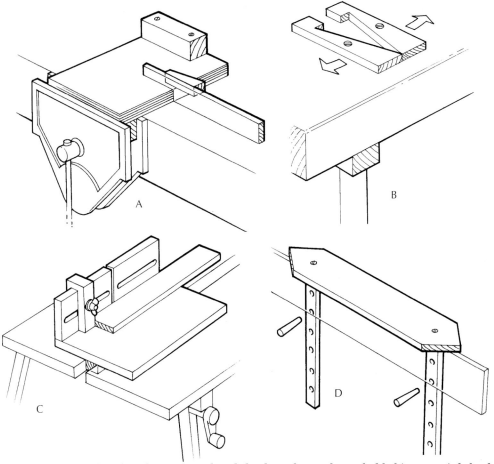

Fig. 20 Some simple bench aids: a: use a bench hook and a wedge to hold thin material, b: this pivoting arrangement will grip your work; c: a simple, adjustable length guide; d: another mitre guide.

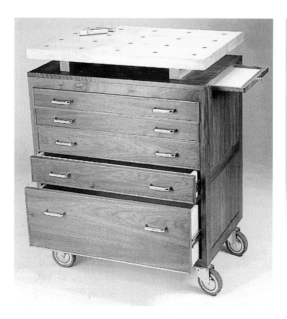

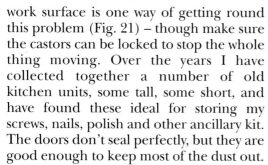

Fig. 21 A useful mobile bench. (BriMarc Associates)

Fig. 22 A large, traditional style tool storage box. (BriMarc Associates)

work surface is one way of getting round this problem (Fig. 21) – though make sure the castors can be locked to stop the whole thing moving. Over the years I have collected together a number of old kitchen units, some tall, some short, and have found these ideal for storing my screws, nails, polish and other ancillary kit. The doors don't seal perfectly, but they are good enough to keep most of the dust out.

Plans are available from various sources to make tool storage boxes in traditional

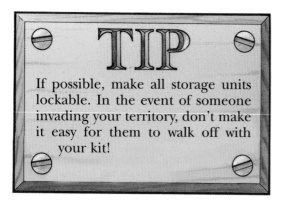

TIP

If possible, make all storage units lockable. In the event of someone invading your territory, don't make it easy for them to walk off with your kit!

style (Figs. 22 and 23). These are designed for use in the workshop principally, although they are portable – albeit with some effort – for use on site as well. It is possible to improvise, however: when I first started moonlighting many years ago I cadged an old ammunition box belonging to my father. I fitted it out with a sliding drawer and various small boxes, and fixed a couple of catches in the lid for my saws. Although heavy, it was also useful to use as a small bench; I'd attached a couple of wooden straps across the top. I could lock this box and leave it on site if necessary – and I painted it red so everyone knew it was mine! A range of portable tool boxes and storage units are readily available from DIY shops today; if you decide to buy one of these, look at all the individual features and pick the one that best suits you. Furthermore, some of the 'Workmates' now incorporate a small vice fitted to the top of a box, which seems a good idea to me. There are also many different storage units available for the

*Fig. 23 A smaller, traditional toolbox.
(BriMarc Associates)*

smaller items such as nails and screws – although you can buy or make alternatives if you have a limited budget and plenty of time.

For the odd job around the house, or a quick fix on site, a traditional canvas bag is ideal; most will probably have some inner compartments for screws and nails.

A canvas bag will not protect your sharp tools, however, which will slop around and knock against each other, so to avoid damage to your chisels, a tool roll may be required. Most of these are made of canvas or leather, though you should check that the area where the sharp bit lies is strengthened to ensure the blades do not cut through. Saw blades are a different matter, and a 'keep' should protect the teeth; this can be a small plastic tube or box with a cut down it that grips the blade from both sides. Keeps like this are normally supplied with a new saw these days; ask for one if it's not in the package. Alternatively you could make your own, by cutting a groove into a strip of wood to take the teeth, then tying it on with some string (Fig. 25). Planes and other sharp bits of kit should be stored individually in bags; again, canvas is ideal. I have gathered together a collection of old bank cash bags, which are big enough for most of my planes. Basically, as long as the material is strong, anything will do.

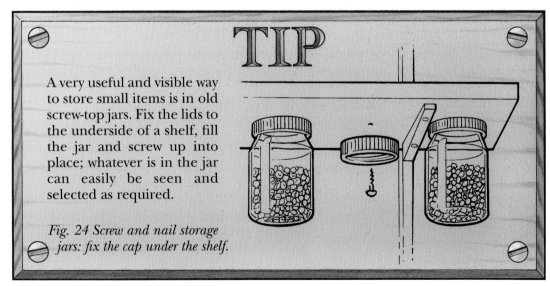

TIP

A very useful and visible way to store small items is in old screw-top jars. Fix the lids to the underside of a shelf, fill the jar and screw up into place; whatever is in the jar can easily be seen and selected as required.

Fig. 24 Screw and nail storage jars: fix the cap under the shelf.

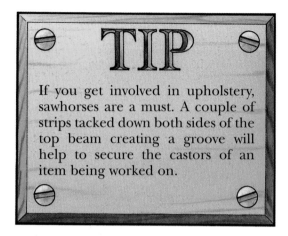

If you get involved in upholstery, sawhorses are a must. A couple of strips tacked down both sides of the top beam creating a groove will help to secure the castors of an item being worked on.

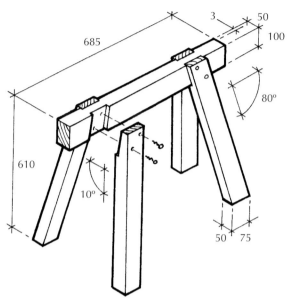

Fig. 26 How to make a simple sawhorse.

SAWHORSES AND STEP-UPS

A very useful addition to any workshop is a pair of sawhorses, as these can take the larger pieces of timber, sheet materials or other big workpieces that a workbench may not be able to handle. They are easy, simple to construct and, in their basic form, take up little space (Fig. 26). There are ranges of different types of sawhorse that you can make. Useful additions include a fixed tray underneath to take tools, and adjustable heights (Fig. 27).

When my wife and I started renovating houses a number of years ago we hired a local builder who was full of bright ideas. One day, when he was plastering a ceiling, I spotted some milk crates he was using. He had cut the locating lugs off the top and turned them over – and these were his

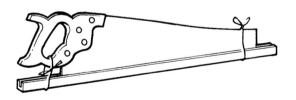

Fig. 25 Protect your saw's teeth with this simple, grooved guard or 'keep'.

'step-ups'. They were just the right height to give him that extra reach to apply the plaster, and were easily kicked around the floor to a new position. I took the idea a bit further and added a flat plywood surface to what was the bottom. These I have found invaluable over the years: whenever I need a bit more height to sit something on, want to reach further – or even do some plastering, they are most useful. A pair is good, four is ideal – and six extravagant!

TOOL STARTER KITS

My father was my first source of tools: we started out by 'sharing' his kit, which was limited, but I gradually took over certain items and claimed them as my own. Others were returned as up-dated kit was purchased. I can still remember my first powered drill, a white-bodied Black and Decker with gold-painted metal parts: it had three speeds and a hammer action,

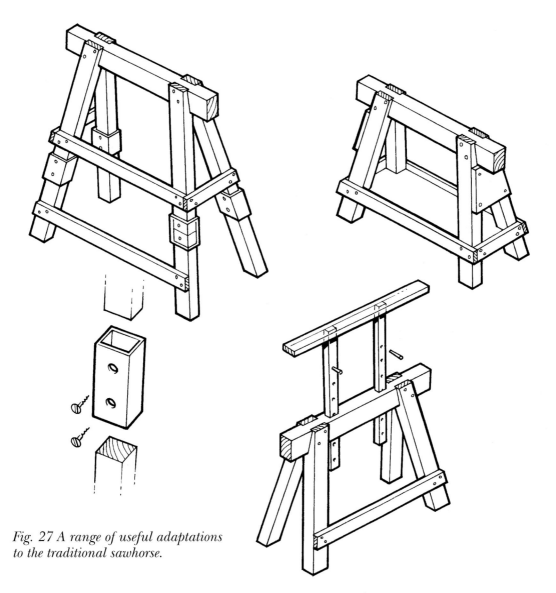

Fig. 27 A range of useful adaptations to the traditional sawhorse.

and was quite expensive at the time. In the end it was money well spent, however, because it must have lasted about fifteen years.

I still have a number of tools that formed part of my original tool kit. The bevel-edged chisels are, admittedly, quite a bit shorter, and the tenon saw is in need of attention, but the majority have endured and been added to. My first ripsaw was made by our company's saw doctor: he took the handle off a worn-out saw and made a new blade. I made my first carpenter's mallet from a chunk of beech. Eventually the head went, but the handle survives today with at least the third or fourth home-made head. And although I now have more than one, my first claw hammer is still in daily use. I have changed the handle several times, but it is a nicely balanced tool that I expect to have in my kit for a long time yet.

Finally, it pays to be selective, and to take time over the choice of tools you buy. Naturally there will be some that wear out, break or get lost, but there is no reason why most of them should not last for years. If I were starting out again today I would go round the local sales and auctions, because there is a huge amount of second-hand kit available. The only tools to avoid – unless you know where they came from – are powered tools; but even new, these don't have to be extortionate in price: keep your eyes open for special offers, closing down sales and old stock clearance sales, and look in the woodworking press magazines and the local classified ads section to see what's available. Nowadays you don't have to pay top price for anything.

Here are some ideas for a basic starter kit that won't be too expensive!

SAWS

You'll probably need two or three. Firstly a universal hard-point saw with six to eight or possibly ten teeth per inch (tpi), or points per inch (ppi); this will be useful for ripping down material and, if you are careful, cutting across the grain. A tenon saw with a brass or metal back is a must; these will have ten to fourteen tpi. For the curved shapes a coping saw is also useful.

HAMMERS

I would suggest that initially you equip yourself with a claw hammer, as they can draw as well as drive nails. A mid-weight one of 10–12oz (280–340g) will cover most of your requirements. To complement this consider a smaller cross-pein hammer for driving panel pins, tacks and small nails; a good size is 3½–4oz (100–115g).

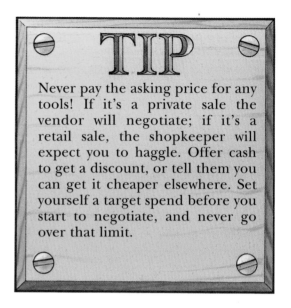

Never pay the asking price for any tools! If it's a private sale the vendor will negotiate; if it's a retail sale, the shopkeeper will expect you to haggle. Offer cash to get a discount, or tell them you can get it cheaper elsewhere. Set yourself a target spend before you start to negotiate, and never go over that limit.

CHISELS

To start with, three or four bevel-edged chisels should be enough for most purposes, say, a 6mm, 10mm and a 12mm; if you can stretch to it, include a 3mm and a 18mm. Remember you can make a bigger hole with a smaller chisel but you can't make a small hole with a big chisel! Impact-resistant plastic handles are best, because you can then use the claw hammer, with care! Choose a range from one supplier that you can add to; it's always nice to have a matching set. You'll also need an oil- or wetstone to sharpen them (these are relatively inexpensive); choose a combination one that has two grades of abrasive, fine and coarse.

SCREWDRIVERS

Two or three of these will be enough for most needs: a small to medium and a large straight tip for slotted screws, and a medium-sized 'Phillips' or 'Pozidrive' to cover most of the other types of screws. Avoid handles with ridges that claim to give better grip: I can assure you these produce blisters! The best handle is a smooth, slightly elliptical wooden one; these can be used all day without causing too many problems.

DRILLS

I have a small hand drill and a brace, and an electric drill in my kit, but I rarely use the first two because the latter covers most of my needs. At the outset, therefore, it might be best to equip yourself with the electric version and add the others later. It is important to consider the type of work you will be doing, too, as this will probably dictate which is most suitable. Choose an electric drill with a range of speeds; this will be helpful when cutting into different materials. A hammer action is not crucial because most masonry bits will still operate without, albeit more slowly. You'll need some drill bits to suit whatever drill you have purchased. Some universal High Speed Steel – HSS – bits are a must, and usually come in sets of various sizes. Countersunk and plug-cutting bits are also very useful.

PLANES

A simple smoothing plane would be my initial choice. A 50mm-wide blade, or possibly 65mm, is best, though take the width of your oil- or wetstone into account. Rebating and grooving planes can follow later, or even a router when you can afford it!

SQUARES AND RULES

A combination square that can be used for both try and mitre squaring is a good choice; some also have spirit levels and a scriber included. Otherwise you must have a traditional try square for marking out: a 125–150mm is best. The cheapest steel retractable tape measure will only be 2m long, but should be sufficient for most jobs; remember that for accurate measuring you should avoid using the end of the tape as they always get damaged. A 150mm or 300mm steel rule is also very useful for those finer measurements.

ODDS AND ENDS

If you want a bradawl, then make one yourself from an old screwdriver: just grind or file a sharp point onto it. A nail punch can be made from a 100mm or 150mm nail: just file the tip off it. Old hacksaw blades make excellent marking and cutting knives: wrap tape round a couple of strips of wood on each side of the blade to make the handle. You could also make a marking gauge yourself, except there are plenty of good, cheap ones around if you look for them. Pliers, or preferably pinchers, are also very useful to have in your kit.

— 3 —

KNOCKING, SCREWING AND DRILLING

This chapter describes a range of tools, their application and uses. They have been hammer-graded on a one-to-five scale to show which are the most essential, five hammers indicating the most practical and desirable tools to buy initially on a limited budget.

HAMMERS, NAILERS AND MALLETS

Hammers are so commonplace we almost take them for granted and, not surprisingly, there are many different versions. Mallets are a bit more basic and tend to be used less often, or for specific purposes. When buying a hammer with a

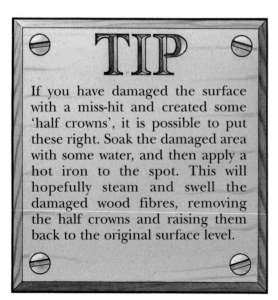

TIP

If you have damaged the surface with a miss-hit and created some 'half crowns', it is possible to put these right. Soak the damaged area with some water, and then apply a hot iron to the spot. This will hopefully steam and swell the damaged wood fibres, removing the half crowns and raising them back to the original surface level.

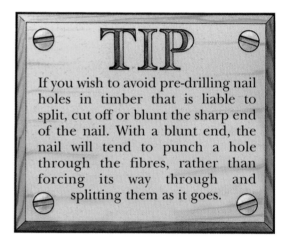

TIP

If you wish to avoid pre-drilling nail holes in timber that is liable to split, cut off or blunt the sharp end of the nail. With a blunt end, the nail will tend to punch a hole through the fibres, rather than forcing its way through and splitting them as it goes.

wooden handle, or a mallet, be sure to look at the grain of the wood carefully: it should be straight and clear, without any knots or deviations. Also, short-grained or cross-grained handles will split and break easily. Traditionally these handles are made from hickory because it is strong, flexible and impact-resistant.

When using any striking tool, there are a few fundamental rules to follow that will make life easier. To take full advantage of the weight of your hammer and its driving power, grip the handle firmly at the end. Start the nail off with a light tap, and swing from the elbow to drive it home. Always look at the nail, not the hammer head – you'll miss otherwise! If the surface into which the nail is being driven must not be damaged, then you must stop before the nail is fully driven home; use a nail punch – or, as it should be called, a 'set' – for finishing off the last bit.

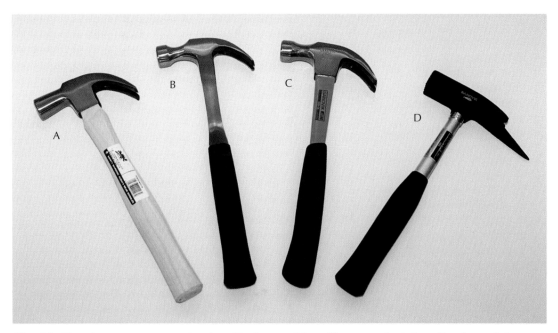

Fig. 28 Claw hammers: a: wooden handle; b: metal handle; c: synthetic handle; d: special 'carpenter's' hammer.

Sometimes the hardened striking face of the hammer is damaged. If this is slight, then grind out or grind back the face, taking care not to overheat it and thus lose its temper. Shiny striking faces should be avoided: use some coarse-grit sandpaper or emery cloth to rough up the surface. Don't let your hammer go rusty, and clean any muck and glue off before putting it away. Some linseed oil applied to wooden handles will help prevent these drying out and becoming loose. If a handle does need re-wedging, use wood first and a metal one to finish off (these metal wedges can be bought in packs at most DIY sheds).

CLAW HAMMER

Sometimes called the 'American' claw hammer, this is probably the most commonly used and easily recognized hammer around today. It comes in a variety of shapes and sizes, with a wooden,

metal or synthetic handle (Fig. 28). The claw hammer is designed for use when constructing framing on a building site, but obviously it can be used in the workshop as a general purpose tool if no other is available.

Claw hammers come in a range of weights and sizes, and it is important that you choose one that feels comfortable,

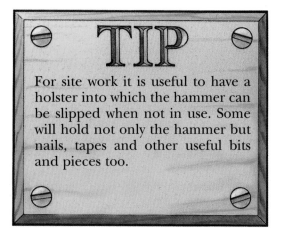

TIP

For site work it is useful to have a holster into which the hammer can be slipped when not in use. Some will hold not only the hammer but nails, tapes and other useful bits and pieces too.

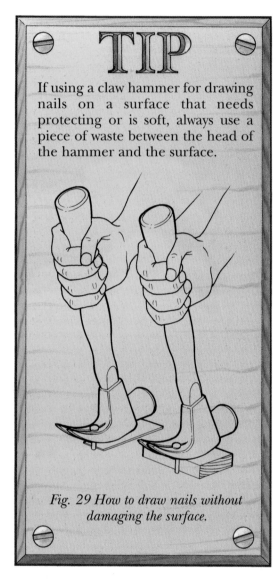

Fig. 29 How to draw nails without damaging the surface.

BALL-PEIN HAMMER

The 'pein' of the hammer is the end of the head opposite the striking head, and in this case it is rounded (Fig. 30d and 31c). Not so commonly found in the workshop today, these hammers are useful as a general-purpose tool. Naturally you will not be able to draw nails, but the ball pein can be used for light metalworking functions such as rounding over rivets or studs.

CROSS-PEIN HAMMER

This is the other most commonly found and useful hammer for the workshop. It comes in a variety of sizes, and today is most often found in a 'Warrington' (Fig. 30b/c), or possibly the alternative 'London' or 'Exeter' pattern (Fig. 30a). Most cabinet makers will have two or three different sizes: the smallest, usually 3½oz (100g), is used for light work with pins and

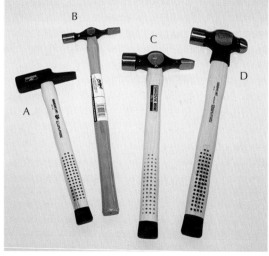

Fig. 30 A range of hammers: a: joiner's 'London' style; b: lightweight cross-pein 'Warrington' style; c: similar heavy weight; d: ball-pein hammer.

and that suits the purpose for which you intend it. A good all-round weight is probably between 10–14oz (280–390g). However, if a lot of heavy constructional work is to be done, then an 18oz (500g) or heavier would be more suitable. In fact too heavy a hammer is no more tiring if used all day than one that is too light, since the latter needs more effort to drive the nails home. The claw action is most useful for pulling or straightening nails.

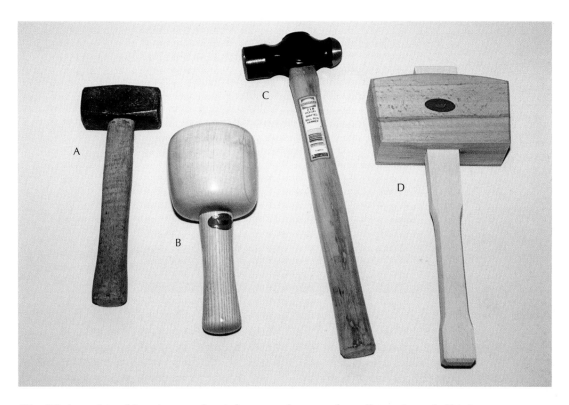

Fig. 31 A variety of knockers: a: lump hammer; b: carver's mallet; c: large ball-pein; d: carpenter's mallet.

brads, and the mid-sized version at 6–8oz (170–225g) is also very useful. If you want one for heavy work, choose a weight over 16oz (450g). The cross-pein is mostly used for starting, or setting, the nail (Fig. 32); once this has been done, swop over to the main striking face. It is quite useful for getting into, and striking in, confined spaces. The cross-pein end of the heavier ones can also be used as a small veneer hammer, to squeeze out excess glue in repair jobs.

CARPENTER'S MALLET

This mallet is most useful for knocking joints together (Fig. 31d), and for work with chisels, as its wooden head is less likely to damage the top of the chisel

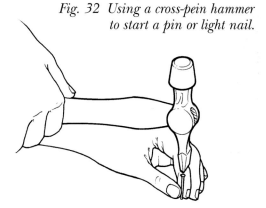

Fig. 32 Using a cross-pein hammer to start a pin or light nail.

when it strikes it. All faces should be tapered in from the top of the mallet head slightly, so that all four faces can be used as and when necessary. Generally sold by size, as measured across the widest face of the head, something between 125–150mm

35

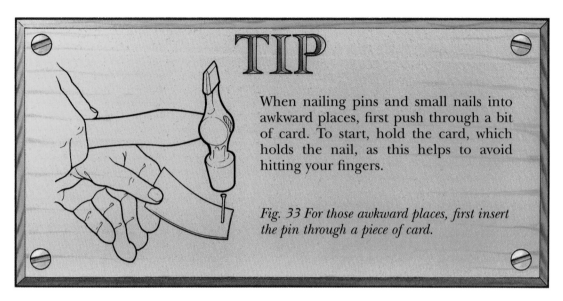

When nailing pins and small nails into awkward places, first push through a bit of card. To start, hold the card, which holds the nail, as this helps to avoid hitting your fingers.

Fig. 33 For those awkward places, first insert the pin through a piece of card.

will be most appropriate. When buying new, avoid mallet heads with straight grain if possible, because these tend to split and break up more quickly than one with interlocking grain. Shop-bought mallets are usually made from beech. If you are going to make your own, try to pick a medium- to heavyweight timber for the head – apple is thought to be good. Use ash for the handle if possible, or failing that, beech.

CARVER'S MALLET

Round rather than square, the woodcarver's mallet will not deflect the carving chisel if a miss-hit is struck (Fig. 31b). Two sizes are useful: 16oz (450g) and 32oz (900g), the lighter one for controlled tapping, and the heavier one for bulk waste removal, stab or stop cuts. The most popular material for the heads is lignum vitae, a heavy, hard, exotic timber that does not split easily and has good impact resistance as well. Some lighter weight mallets are made from beech, however these types should be avoided because they do not last so long – the surface of the head tends to

crumple and then split away. If making your own, use a heavy hardwood if no lignum vitae is available. Smaller, but just as heavy, bronze mallets are available today; these are quite expensive, but have the advantage of longevity if in constant use.

LUMP HAMMER

Not really a woodworker's tool, these can be useful at times (Fig. 31a). If a particularly difficult, but sturdy, frame or joint needs some persuasion, this is the

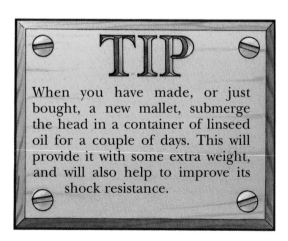

When you have made, or just bought, a new mallet, submerge the head in a container of linseed oil for a couple of days. This will provide it with some extra weight, and will also help to improve its shock resistance.

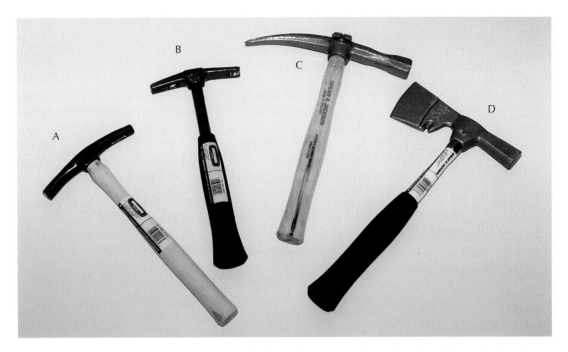

Fig. 34 Specialist hammers: a: magnet upholstery hammer with wooden handle; b: similar, but with a metal handle; c: slater's hammer for punching, drawing and nailing; d: hatchet with a hammerhead.

tool for the job – for instance, when assembling studding for partition walls it will knock the most difficult piece into place. It can also be used behind the striking area to give support as nails are driven home.

CABRIOLE HAMMER

This is a specialist hammer used in the upholstery trade (Fig. 34a/b): the head is fairly long and curved, with a claw at one end for drawing tacks; some have integral metal bars down the handle to provide extra strength when used for this purpose. The striking face should not be too large, to avoid causing excess damage to a polished surface should a miss-hit occur. Most are magnetized so the user can pick up and start tacks with one hand. As with the claw hammer, put some waste between

the head and the workpiece if the surface needs protecting.

VENEER HAMMER

Not a hammer in the true sense of the word, this is a specialist bit of kit for traditional veneering techniques (Fig.35): it is not used to strike with, but to squeeze out excess glue from between the veneer and groundwork. Most importantly the leading edge should be fully smoothed and rounded to avoid damaging the veneer surface.

In addition to all the traditional-style hammers, a great many specialist types are now to be found, such as the slater's hammer (Fig. 34c), and the lath, or plasterer's hammer (Fig. 34d) which has a hatchet on one end. The list is endless; however, three or four will do most things.

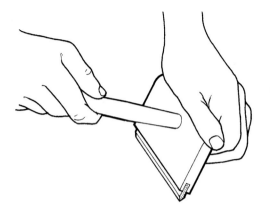

Fig. 35 A simple veneer 'hammer'.

Fig. 36 One way to start off the drawing process; never use metal on metal.

NAIL PULLERS

We will now look at tools that are able to draw nails out, rather than drive them in! There will be times when nails need to be pulled from the best face of a piece of furniture, and in these circumstances the nail head will have to be exposed. Cutting round it with care will ensure that after the nail is extracted, the surface can be made good. Most of us will have a nail puller of sorts in the toolbox – if not, the humble claw hammer can be used as a last resort (Fig. 36). Note that it is imperative never to hit the striking face of the pulling hammer with another hammer or metal object; this is because the faces are tempered and will shed dangerous splinters if treated in this way – and it will also ruin the hammers! If you have no alternative, use a mallet, and at worst, punch the nail away into the wood and make good the surface.

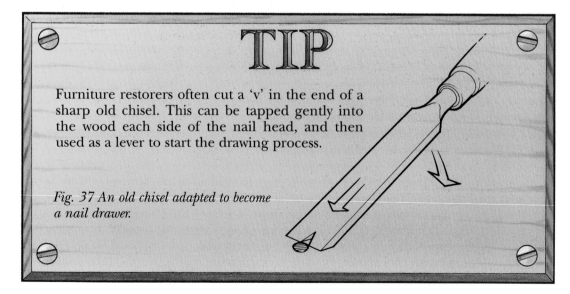

TIP

Furniture restorers often cut a 'v' in the end of a sharp old chisel. This can be tapped gently into the wood each side of the nail head, and then used as a lever to start the drawing process.

Fig. 37 An old chisel adapted to become a nail drawer.

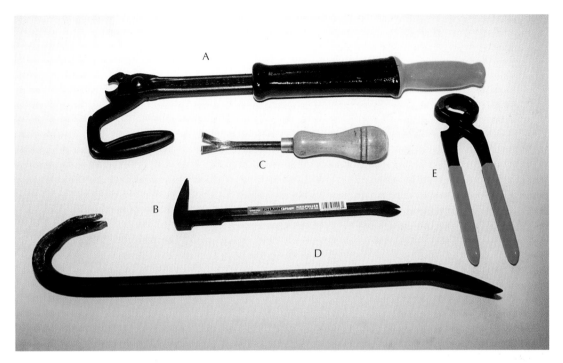

Fig. 38 Various drawing tools: a: heavy duty nail puller – the weight slides up and down to drive the jaws into the wood; b: double-ended nail puller that can be driven in; c: upholstery tack puller; d: wrecking bar used to lever and draw; e: pair of pincers.

HEAVY DUTY PULLER

This purpose-made nail puller has an integral sliding weight fitted to the handle (Fig. 38a): the jaws are positioned each side of the nail head, and the weight is then slammed down; this action drives the jaws into the wood and, once far enough in, the nail can be levered out. This is an industrial tool used for taking apart packing cases and pallets, and is useful but not essential.

DUAL PURPOSE PULLERS

Some forged steel nail pullers have a head at each end of the shaft to carry out different functions. The one illustrated (Fig. 38b) has a simple nail or tack remover at one end: using a block of wood, this will pull nails that have been started, or will lever tacks out of upholstery. The other end is cranked and will easily pull out exposed nail heads; also, when the nail is below the surface, this end can be driven in until the sharp jaws grip the shaft of the nail so it can be pulled. Makers claim that this tool will pull all types of nail, including headless ones. They are available in various lengths: pick the one that most suits your application.

SMALL NAIL AND TACK PULLER

This tool is especially useful for upholstery work (Fig. 38c); it is fairly lightweight, so will not take abuse. Hand pressure is used to force the head under webbing or material to lift out the offending tack. It can be used for small nails, but on face surfaces a block of wood should be used as protection; this also helps the lifting action.

WRECKING BARS

The wrecking bar is one of those tools that is not often used, but is handy to have around (see Fig. 38d). Made from forged steel, it has an angled lever on one end for prying open lids on cases and suchlike, and the other is rounded and culminates in a set of jaws. This latter end is used for nail pulling, and because of the rounded shape, it can easily pull large nails right out. Any face surfaces need protecting well before use.

PINCERS

Another very useful bit of kit for the tool-box (Fig. 38e): these are indispensable for pulling smaller nails. Some makers incorporate a tack puller into the end of one of the handles, which makes this tool even more versatile. The jaws are generally bevelled to allow for a better grip on the nail. Some of the cheaper ones will need some smoothing of the faces adjacent to the wood; often the casting has not been filed away completely.

SCREWDRIVERS

The humble 'turnscrew', as it used to be called, is much abused and often misused. My workshop contains a large number of screwdrivers accumulated over many years, though inevitably there have been casualties along the way – often caused by hitting the handle with a hammer whilst trying to lever something, which generally ends up with it disintegrating or splitting.

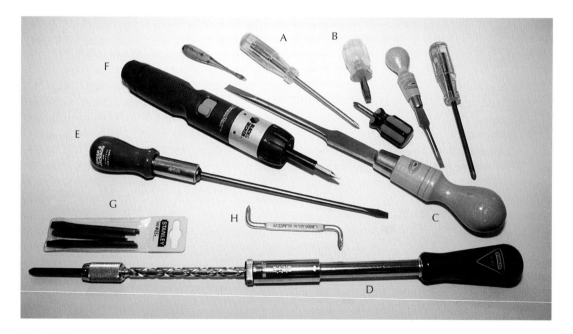

Fig. 39 A range of screwdrivers: a: 'Phillips' super-grip handle; b: stubby, straight tip; c: cabinet screwdriver with wooden handle; d: 'Yankee'; e: ratchet; f: battery-powered; g: bits for the Yankee; h: small, cranked screwdriver.

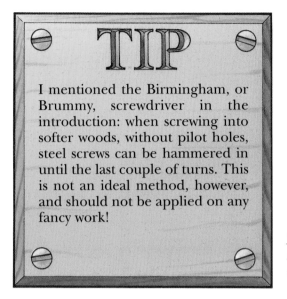

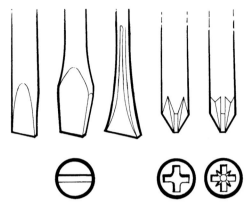

Fig. 40 Screwdriver tips: a: straight parallel; b: straight tapered; c: straight flared; d: Phillips; e: pozi, and/or supa drive.

Others have been around for a long time and are like comfortable old friends.

Almost as important as the business end of the traditional screwdriver is the handle, the significance of which I learned through painful experience: an early commission many years ago called for a number of screws to be driven home, and at that time I had only one screwdriver for straight-slotted screws, with an old wooden handle that had a few chunks missing out of it. Soon after I started, the first of several blisters appeared around the palm of my hand – and were they sore afterwards! By the next job I had smoothed off all the imperfections in the handle, and it was reasonably serviceable thereafter. Over the years I have had similar problems with plastic handles that claim to be 'super grip' (Figs. 39a, b): they are fine for a few screws, but not for a big job.

A cabinet screwdriver has the most comfortable handle (Fig. 39c): normally fully rounded, elliptical or with a slightly flattened main body, they can be used for sustained screwing. If, however, you want to open tins, use the screwdriver as a chisel, or start stuck screws, then buy a cheap, plastic-handled version that can be knocked around. Powered screwdrivers will, of course, remove any chance of blisters anyway; lighter-weight ones will look vaguely similar to a traditional screwdriver (Fig. 39f). For heavy-duty work they will look like a standard electric drill, with or without a cord.

These days we are all familiar with the two main types of screw, namely slotted and cross-headed. Traditional straight-slotted screws are widely available and still in demand, especially in brass. The cross-

headed screw was developed to provide better grip, in that there is more surface area for the tip of the screwdriver to make contact with; within the latter type there is a number of variations, and it is critically important to match the type of screw head to the correct screwdriver (Fig. 40).

Whatever the type of screwdriver, whether hand or power driven, matching the tip to the screw head will ensure a successful drive in most cases – for this reason you will find a number of screwdrivers in most workshops. Note the following, however, when driving or removing screws with straight slots: using a screwdriver that is too large will score the surface of the wood; and using one that is too small will damage the slot (Fig. 41a/b). If yours is too large you can make it smaller (Fig. 41c), but only as a last resort. You can't make a screwdriver tip larger, and if stuck, may have to accept some damage to the screw. One advantage of straight-slotted screws is that they can often be restored to use with a hacksaw and file.

Damaging a cross-headed screw is of more serious concern, and in most instances will occur when a powered screwdriver is being used with the wrong

Fig. 41 Use the right size screwdriver for the job; a large screwdriver can be made to fit.

sized driving tip. There is no real excuse for this because quick changeover tips of various sizes are readily available (Fig. 43). Typically, when this does happen, the tip will start to spin round in the screw recess when resistance to the drive starts to increase, the result being a rounded

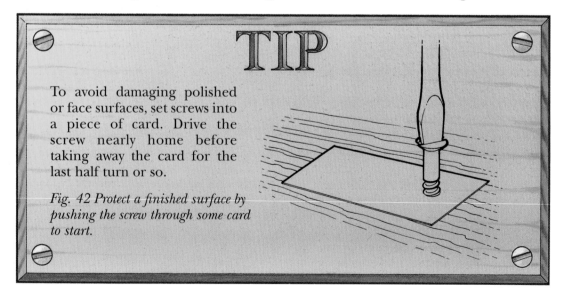

TIP

To avoid damaging polished or face surfaces, set screws into a piece of card. Drive the screw nearly home before taking away the card for the last half turn or so.

Fig. 42 Protect a finished surface by pushing the screw through some card to start.

Fig. 43 Some screwdriver tips with a range of quick changeover bits. a: The holder into which the bits are fitted.

recess into which nothing fits! Holding the screwdriver at a slight angle will also help to dislodge the tip as the screw is driven, and results in the same damage – and if you have to extract the screw you'll be really unhappy! The tip of the screwdriver will also suffer, in that the sharp corners necessary to make good contact with the screw recess will be rounded – so the next time it's used, the problem will be exacerbated. Therefore to reduce frustration, and to ensure that screws perform in the way they should, be sure to match them with the appropriate screwdriver tip.

It is very difficult to restore the tip shape to a cross-driver, however it can often be achieved with a straight one; this is made reasonably easy with a bench grinder. Re-grind the two wide faces first – slightly hollow is ideal – then tidy the sides and square off the tip; try not to overheat it because this will affect the temper of the metal. If a bench grinder is not available, then you will have to use hand files and bench stones.

It is important to position yourself correctly when driving screws. Having located the screwdriver snugly into the screw head, ensure that your wrist and forearm are straight in line with it; to exert pressure your body should be above, with your weight helping to drive the screw. Working from the side or below is always difficult. You may need to position yourself in such a way that support is provided to your back, especially the driving shoulder.

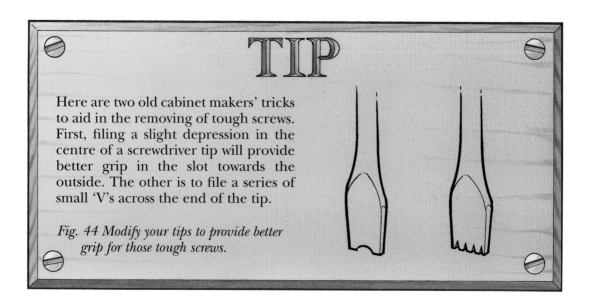

TIP

Here are two old cabinet makers' tricks to aid in the removing of tough screws. First, filing a slight depression in the centre of a screwdriver tip will provide better grip in the slot towards the outside. The other is to file a series of small 'V's across the end of the tip.

Fig. 44 Modify your tips to provide better grip for those tough screws.

The range of screwdrivers available is very wide, in type, size and shape, and most workshops will need at least six to be fully efficient. Think about matching the tip type and size to the screws you will use for different jobs, and this will help you to match the most likely screwdriver to each application.

CABINET SCREWDRIVER

In my opinion it is absolutely vital to include in any tool kit two or three cabinet screwdrivers of different sizes. These generally have a bulbous, slightly elliptical handle (Fig. 39c), and a rounded shaft that culminates in a flared or straight tip. The

Fig. 45 A 'London' pattern screwdriver with flat handle sides.

shape of the handle ensures comfort, and also provides a large surface area to give good grip. The cabinet screwdriver is readily available in both wood, and compounds such as plastic, resin or polypropylene. There is also a wide range of lengths, therefore choose, ideally, a small, a medium and a large one for your collection.

LONDON PATTERN SCREWDRIVER

This is a variation on the cabinet version, or vice versa (Fig. 45); with the handle flattened on both sides, it provides tremendous grip for those really tough jobs. Traditionally the shaft is made from flat steel with a straight or flared tip. Not so readily available nowadays, they can occasionally be found in local sales and auctions; if you come across any good ones they are worth the investment.

POINTED TIP SCREWDRIVERS

You will probably need a range of these to fit Phillips, pozi- and super-drive screws, and probably two of each. Try and buy the same sort of screws for use in the workshop every time, as this will limit the number of drivers required. Most of these screwdrivers can be found with the cabinet handles described above. There is also a vast range of what are called 'engineer's' screwdrivers (Fig. 39a): they have fluted handles, the sort I don't like, and may also be shaped to fit a spanner at the base of the handle. The theory here is that extra leverage can be applied with a spanner in cases where access is difficult, or screws are stuck. In my opinion they have their place, but are not for general use in a woodworker's workshop.

STUBBY SCREWDRIVERS

These are most useful when trying to get into small gaps (Fig. 39b); the handle grips come in a variety of styles. In this case the fluted version is probably as good as the round one; hopefully you will only be using them to extract or drive in a couple of screws. Slight variations on the theme are the cranked or offset screwdrivers (Fig. 39f): these also have their place, but as you would expect, are difficult to use.

RATCHET SCREWDRIVERS

These are generally available with both straight and pointed tips (Fig. 39e), and come in a variety of sizes. Gears are housed within a cylinder at the top of the shaft, and are controlled by a small thumb slide. This ratchet control allows you to both drive and withdraw screws without changing grip. The thumb slide allows you to lock the shaft to turn clockwise or anti-clockwise. The shaft can also be locked off, normally the central position, turning the screwdriver into a conventional, fixed action one. Apart from the cabinet drivers, I personally find these the most useful in my workshop.

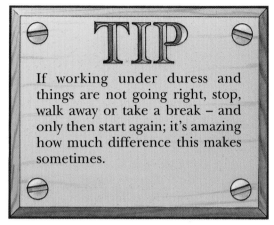

TIP

If working under duress and things are not going right, stop, walk away or take a break – and only then start again; it's amazing how much difference this makes sometimes.

YANKEE SCREWDRIVERS

This is an American design now some one hundred years old (Fig. 39d). It employs a special double-spiral shaft action that is turned by pumping the handle: the pump action, and how quickly it is depressed, determine the speed of the drive. Like the ratchet screwdriver, it can be set to drive in, or to remove screws, and it, too, can be locked off. This last feature turns the action into a conventional fixed drive, either when the handle is fully extended, or when it is depressed; for stability the latter is best, for reach the former. The sophisticated Yankees made today can also become a ratchet screwdriver, and to make them even more versatile they are fitted with a chuck at the end of the shaft. This chuck will take a variety of different tips (see Fig. 39g), allowing for quick changeover, and ease of matching tip size to the appropriate screw.

A Yankee must be used carefully. When driving screws home it is important to hold the chuck steady with your spare hand to ensure that the tip of the screwdriver does not jump out of the recess.

These screwdrivers are very useful and highly versatile, and for that alone they must score highly; they have always been

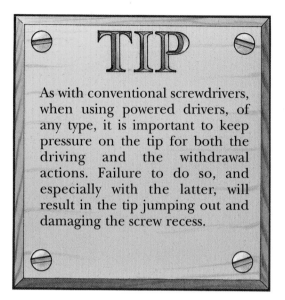

As with conventional screwdrivers, when using powered drivers, of any type, it is important to keep pressure on the tip for both the driving and the withdrawal actions. Failure to do so, and especially with the latter, will result in the tip jumping out and damaging the screw recess.

popular amongst the professionals, especially those working on site a lot. Having said that, today, however, they are slightly losing their place to the mass of cordless professional drivers now available.

POWERED SCREWDRIVERS

These are becoming increasingly popular. Air-line and cabled electric drills have for a long time had the capacity to be turned into screwdrivers for long, repetitive work, and nowadays they can be fitted with speed controls and clutches to ensure the screws are not damaged or over-tensioned. With the enhancement of cordless tool battery design and technology, the humble screwdriver is being put to one side for limited use only.

There are many dedicated powered screwdrivers on the market today. In design they tend to look like a conventional screwdriver (Fig. 39f) or a pistol-grip electric drill, and typical features will include forward and reverse drives, variable speeds and a clutch to ensure that screws are not snapped off.

Some of those with an in-line handle will also allow you to lock off the shaft for use as a conventional screwdriver. This is useful to apply the final pressure when driving home or, in reverse, to start the withdrawal action. Both will ensure the batteries are not strained and drained too quickly.

Powered drivers have really become a necessity in most workshops today, having all the features of conventional screwdrivers, coupled with speed of use and ease of action. They are not, however, the ultimate answer, and must be used with care – I have seen some beautiful work ruined by too hasty use of these tools. Once again, consider carefully all the features of any driver you are thinking of buying, and be sure it suits your needs and available funds.

DRILLS, BRACES AND BITS

My first (borrowed) drill was a large, hand-driven one with a broken breastplate, with drill bits that were old

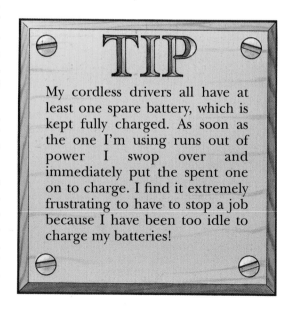

My cordless drivers all have at least one spare battery, which is kept fully charged. As soon as the one I'm using runs out of power I swop over and immediately put the spent one on to charge. I find it extremely frustrating to have to stop a job because I have been too idle to charge my batteries!

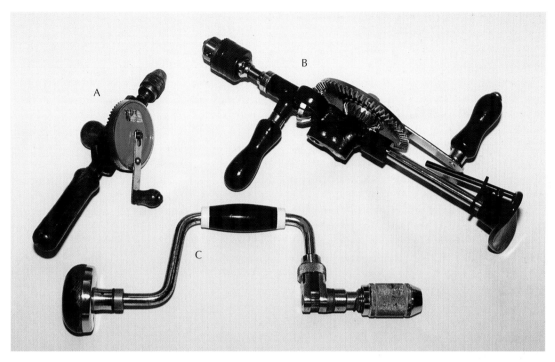

Fig. 46 Some hand-boring kit: a: small wheel brace; b: large wheel brace with chest plate; c: ratchet brace.

and blunt, and with a limited variation in sizes. Some of the centre bits were cut down versions, and we didn't have a brace so the square tapered drive had been cut off! All needed attention. As soon as I could afford it I bought a reversible brace and a few auger bits, and these I have added to over the years. An electric drill joined the team shortly thereafter, which was a tremendous leap forwards; now I hardly ever use the hand-powered kit.

This is not to say that I have no time for hand drills, and don't see them as a necessity in a modern workshop. It just happens that the range of powered tools I have collected covers the vast majority of my needs, and the type of work that I do only calls for hand-controlled drilling occasionally – and when it does, I revert to the tools for the job. Basically, if you have a tool that is quicker and more efficient, then use it – I don't see the point of

drilling all day by hand when I can accomplish the same amount of work in half an hour with an electric drill.

HAND DRILLS

These come in a variety of shapes and sizes, the most common being those that are sometimes called 'wheel braces' (Fig. 46a and b); cut-down versions with enclosed gearing (Fig. 47a), and some that look very similar to a powered drill (Fig. 47b) are also found. Whatever the size and shape, they all have a similar function. The gearing that provides power is driven by the rotation of the handle; this is a positive action, therefore the drive can be both clockwise and anticlockwise. The body gear, or pinion, is tapered to fit the opposing gear on the handle drive. Cheaper versions come with only one pinion and are more than adequate for light work; however, if you can afford it, buy one that has a double pinion because these tools will tend to be better balanced and last longer.

Opening and closing the usual three-jaw chuck is an easy operation. The outer case is held by one hand, and the driving wheel turned with the other; once hand-tight, the jaws should have sufficient purchase to hold the appropriate drill bits. A side handle is a useful addition for some jobs, although you won't use it a lot. Smaller hand drills will normally take bits up to about 6mm, and should be used for light drilling only. For heavy work a much larger model with a breastplate will be best; these will generally have a chuck that will take up to 12mm diameter bits. The gearing and construction of these larger drills will also allow the use of much bigger bits if required.

BRACES

If you have to make a choice between a brace and a hand drill, then go for the brace (Fig. 46c): for general application in the workshop it is much more useful. The size of hole that can be drilled is restricted only by your own strength – if you can't turn it, you won't drill it! – and the size of available bits to do the job. Rather than gears, the brace is driven from the cranked handle, and as long as you can keep turning it, you will drill a hole.

The basic mechanics of the brace are simple. At the top end there is a free-moving ball head: it does not turn with the frame; wooden heads are the most comfortable. The handle in the centre of the frame is also free moving. The business end is usually fitted with a two-jaw 'hollow shell' chuck; this is designed to grip square-tapered bits that are purpose made. Some of the more sophisticated chucks will be designed with a universal

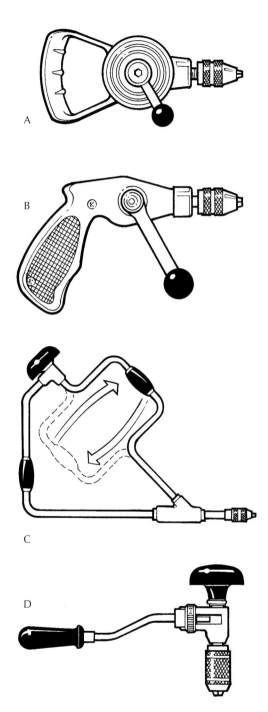

Fig. 47 Variations on a theme: a: wheel brace with enclosed gearing; b: wheel brace with enclosed gearing and pistol grip; c: corner brace; d: joist brace.

48

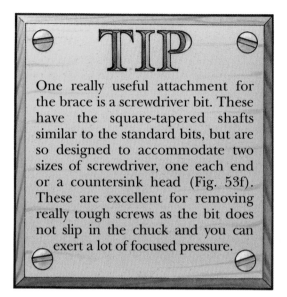

One really useful attachment for the brace is a screwdriver bit. These have the square-tapered shafts similar to the standard bits, but are so designed to accommodate two sizes of screwdriver, one each end or a countersink head (Fig. 53f). These are excellent for removing really tough screws as the bit does not slip in the chuck and you can exert a lot of focused pressure.

action and can have three or four jaws; this type of chuck is able to take round and morse-tapered drill bits as well as the standard square tapered ones.

Braces are classified by the size of sweep, the full turning circle of the centre handle. This is most commonly about 250mm, but larger and smaller ones are available, the latter being particularly useful in confined spaces. Large ones should also be more robust because greater strain is placed on all the components by the increased sweep. A useful addition to any brace is a ratchet action, because this allows the user to work with short strokes, ratchet back, and then continue drilling. A cam ring at the end of the frame, before the chuck, controls this, and can be locked in and out as required. The ratchet comes into its own when working in confined spaces that only allow a short sweep. For difficult places a corner brace (Fig. 47c) might be useful (although I have never seen or used one); or a joist brace (Fig. 47d) for a tight corner job.

Standard braces can be used in both the vertical and horizontal position. When drilling horizontally your stomach can exert pressure on the brace head; and in vertical mode, at the right level, your own head can be used – though try to avoid pulling your hair out!

Braces do have their place in the workshop. Chair makers will often set up more than one, all charged with different sized drill bits, ready to use, to save time changing over the bits. I have to admit that I don't use my ratchet brace too often in the workshop, but generally leave it set up with a 12mm auger bit ready for cutting out plugged screw recesses.

ELECTRIC DRILLS

There are a great many different types and sizes of electric drill available today, and I have very broadly tried to classify them below. In fact all manufacturers will have a range that covers and overlaps this listing, and if you are not careful you will be bewildered by the choice. I have also tried to identify the likely features you might find offered with individual drills; in most cases it will be a combination of many, and you will have to decide what is best for you.

If you are to be involved with a lot of site work, give some consideration to 110 volt-powered kit using a transformer. It is also imperative that both at home and in the workshop a circuit breaker is used. As before, think about the applications you may wish to put the tool to: if a lot of heavy drilling is required, then go up in specification, and if only light work is anticipated, then go down. Ideally you will probably end up with at least two or more drills with features that will accommodate just about all your needs.

The advantages of corded drills are being gradually eroded as battery technology improves. However, the corded version can deliver more power over a sustained period without having to worry about the battery running out, a reassuring feature very definitely in their favour. All my cordless tools have at least two batteries to avoid this eventuality, yet I still pick up a cabled drill for tough jobs.

The manufacturer usually quotes the size of the drill's motor, in wattage; as a general indicator the higher the wattage the more powerful the drill is likely to be. Thus tools capable of continuous heavy duty use will be more expensive, whereas a drill used intermittently need only be a lightweight one. Look carefully at the individual drills on offer in the range you need, paying particular attention to the build quality. You should also check the guarantee. These points, combined with the features, should help guide you towards the best one to buy.

HEAVY DUTY DRILLS

Any drill with a power capacity of 800 watts or more will generally be categorized as heavy duty (Fig. 48a). Common features usually include variable or two-speed motors with lockable trigger, hammer and reverse actions with, maybe, part of the body formed in metal. Because the drill will be used for rough, heavy work, keyless chucks are not normally employed. Using a key in a standard chuck to tighten the bit in place helps to prevent it coming loose during use. Many of the masonry drill bits or chisels used with these drills will have hexagonal shafts for added grip. Specialist demolition percussion drills will have a standard size, hexagonal, quick-changeover chuck into which the bits are directly placed; they are kept there through a variety of methods, but will undoubtedly have some sort of quick release device. Apart from the motor size, the main thing to look out for is the boring capacity. Manufacturers will generally tell you on the packaging the

recommended maximum capacity for wood, steel and concrete – so don't buy something that won't drill the hole size you want.

MEDIUM DUTY DRILLS

Very broadly, power output in this range will be between 600 to 800 watts (Fig. 48b). Standard or keyless chuck capacity will usually be 12mm or 13mm. The most likely features will include hammer and reverse action, variable speeds, and easily adjusted side handles with integrated depth stops. Weight should now be taken into consideration: if you are going to carry this drill around for much of the day, then it does not want to be too heavy. As a guide, most will be 3–5lb (1.5–2.5kg); pick one that feels comfortable at around 4 ½lb (2kg) for most uses.

LIGHTWEIGHT DRILLS

These tools will last a long time if you don't try to use them in industrial applications. Typically they will have a power output of no more than 600 watts, and will weigh about 3lb (1.5kg) (Fig. 48c). Features may be more limited with these smaller drills, but you should still expect two speeds, reverse and maybe hammer action. Chuck capacity is also smaller, in most cases limited to 10mm. When buying in this bracket get as many features as you can for the least amount of money.

CORDLESS DRILLS

Battery technology has advanced in leaps and bounds, and this has ensured an increase in the number of cordless drills available to suit many needs and pockets. Most will be a useful combination between a drill and a driver (Fig. 48e). When you buy, take the drill in hand and feel the

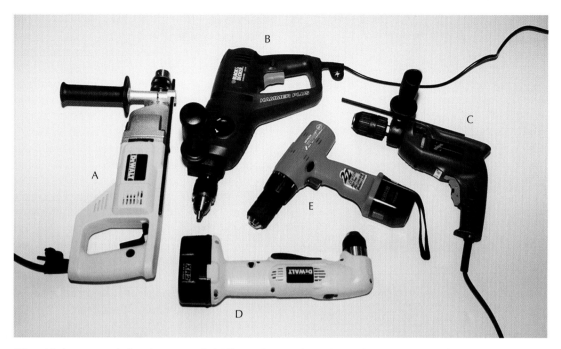

Fig. 48 A range of electric powered drills: a: heavy duty; b: medium duty; c: lightweight; d: right-angle drill; e: cordless drill/driver.

weight and balance – and if it's not comfortable, then don't buy it! The range of features might include two or variable speeds, torque control for driving and removing screws, keyless chucks, and reverse and (sometimes) hammer actions. Basically what you get with a corded drill can be found on a cordless.

Why, then, don't we all buy cordless? The answer is that they are not designed to cover all the applications that a corded drill can handle, and although bigger batteries now weigh about 14 volts or more, they will not handle the really tough jobs that a heavy duty drill will. So the flexibility offered by a cordless drill must be weighed against the required application.

Battery power packs generally come in four sizes: 7.2v, 9.6v, 12v and 14.4v. This dictates the power of the tool, so give some thought to what you want. Until recently most batteries have been Nickel-Cadmium (Ni-Cd); however, they tend not to retain optimum performance if charged. It is my understanding that if a Ni-Cd battery is charged before it is fully discharged then this may affect its charge 'memory', leading to a reduction in the charge capacity. Therefore if you have, or purchase, Ni-Cd battery-powered tools, then run them right out until they are fully discharged before charging them again. And more importantly, don't 'top up' the batteries when you have used them for a little while, as this may result in a permanently lower charge rate! This is why I always have a fully charged spare to hand.

The latest technology uses Nickel Metal Hydride (Ni-MH) batteries, which are claimed not to suffer from the memory loss associated with Ni-Cd batteries. They can therefore be charged at any stage of the proceedings without any long-lasting detrimental effect on their capacity to

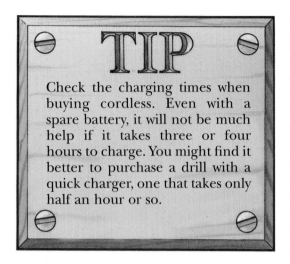

TIP

Check the charging times when buying cordless. Even with a spare battery, it will not be much help if it takes three or four hours to charge. You might find it better to purchase a drill with a quick charger, one that takes only half an hour or so.

retain the charge. Ni-MH battery technology is also said to be better for the environment.

OTHER DRILLS AND THEIR FEATURES

RIGHT-ANGLE DRILLS

I have had a cordless right-angle drill for a number of years, and would not be without it. As support for the rest of the drilling team it can be used for most jobs; in a tight corner it is unbeaten – and by that I mean I can usually get in to drill a hole or tighten a screw when I have a gap of only 120–150mm. There are various makes available with all the associated features that you will find on other powered drills (Fig. 48d), though the most crucial, in my opinion, is the head height: it must be about 100mm or less. If you can afford to have one of these in your tool kit they are well worth the expenditure.

CHUCKS

First of all there are the quick-action chucks that enable the operator to use a standard drill bit of uniform size or shape.

Otherwise there are two main chucks generally available today, the most traditional one being operated with a key; this is inserted into the appropriate locating hole and turned to open or close the jaws. It is always best to finish tightening these chucks by using all the key locating holes in turn, thus ensuring that equal pressure is exerted all round. In more recent years keyless chucks have been developed and are becoming common: with these, holding the outer part of the chuck whilst driving the motor forwards or backwards will tighten or loosen the grip on the inserted tool. These are a great advance as far as speed of changeover and ease of use are concerned; although in hammer mode they might not be quite as efficient as one that is key-tightened.

CONSTANT ELECTRONIC

Some of the more sophisticated drills will have this feature: regardless of the load applied, the drill will maintain constant speed delivery – meaning that it won't slow down when you really lean into it!

HAMMER ACTION

Excellent for knocking holes into masonry of various types. An in-built reciprocating piston delivers several hundred blows per second to aid the boring action. Always use the recommended bits for these drills: if you don't, they will break up. The hammer action should only be used when boring the appropriate materials. A switch or lever will disable the action and return the tool to normal use.

REVERSE ACTION

Most drills will have this feature, and it is an essential for keyless chucks, since without it they won't work! Reverse levers and switches seem to be situated in different places on every model: I like those that are easily accessible to the thumb or forefinger; when they are, you can switch directions easily, without having to fumble about.

SAFETY CLUTCH

These are usually fitted to the heavy duty kit. If a bit becomes jammed during use they will stop and allow the operator to withdraw the bit. This is helpful and avoids any potential damage to the tool or the user.

TORQUE CONTROL

Drill/drivers will generally have torque control fitted: this ensures that when using the tool as a screwdriver, screws cannot be over-screwed, which might lead to them being broken off. Practise a bit before deciding upon the appropriate setting. Not only do they protect the screw, they will protect the operator and the drill by stopping electronically. The control also allows the drill to be set in 'normal' mode, thus performing as any standard drill would.

TWO-SPEED DRILLS

Simple drills will have a two-speed function, which will allow the tool to be used for a range of applications. Depending upon the bit size, slow speeds will be appropriate for metal, and fast for wood.

VARIABLE SPEED DRILLS

This feature is really useful: some drills will have a numbered control to determine the speed setting; others will use trigger pressure. The trigger-controlled feature is great when, for

example, you are starting to drill a hole and you need to be fairly slow, but once away you can speed up. Look out for 'soft start' variable speed drills, which in my opinion are very useful – no matter how much pressure exerted on the trigger they don't start off with a jerk!

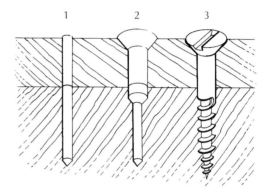

Fig. 49 The correct sequence for drilling pilot and clearance holes.

DRILL BITS

A whole range of different types of drill bit is generally to be found in woodworkers' bags and boxes. They will have a variety of uses, some specific and some universal. The type of material to be bored will determine the size and the purpose of the bore, and this in turn will determine factors affecting the choice of bit. For example, pre-drilling correctly before screwing will use two straight bits and a countersink bit (Fig. 49), all related to the size of screw used. If you are going to use a brace regularly, then the square-tapered bits are a must unless you have a universal chuck that will take straight shanks as well. Simple High Speed Steel (HSS) drill bits are always useful, and probably the cheapest. For clean cutting, a bit with a spur is most efficient. All will need care. A special set will almost certainly come in a box or a roll, in which case always return each bit to its appropriate position, for

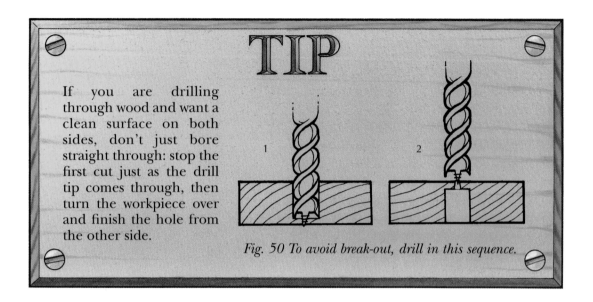

TIP

If you are drilling through wood and want a clean surface on both sides, don't just bore straight through: stop the first cut just as the drill tip comes through, then turn the workpiece over and finish the hole from the other side.

Fig. 50 To avoid break-out, drill in this sequence.

three reasons: first, you'll know if one is missing; second, you'll always know where to find them; and finally, the business end will stay sharper for longer.

ADJUSTABLE BORE BITS

These are often called expansive bits (Fig. 53c) and are generally designed for shallow work, or for boring through thin materials. The wing, or spur, section of the bit can simply be adjusted to produce different diameter holes: all you need is a screwdriver. Expansive bits were traditionally used in a brace with a square taper on the end of the shaft. They are readily available today with straight shafts for use in powered drills. Take care when using them. Also, try not to remove too much waste too quickly, as they jam up easily.

AUGER BITS

These come in a range of different patterns. Although originally designed for use in a brace, most styles are adaptable, with care, for use in powered drills.

* The 'Jennings' pattern auger bit (Figs. 51b and 52a) has a screw point, to help pull the bit through the wood, and a well engineered throat to carry the chips away from the cutting end. These bits are the preferential choice if a clean bore is required.

* The solid centre auger bit also has a screw tip (Figs. 51c and 52b), and for rapid hole-boring these are ideal, the deep throat ensuring that waste chips can get away quickly from the cutting end.

* Multi-speed auger bits have been designed for use in both powered and hand situations (Figs. 51e and 52d): generally with a screw tip and only one spur, these bits are excellent for long, straight holes; the wide 'lands' – the flat surface on the outer spiral – ensures that the bit follows the tip accurately.

* 'Scotch screw-eyed' augers (Fig. 51d) can use any of these bit designs: a wooden handle is pushed through the hole in the end, and you drive them in by hand. As a 'farm boy' I recognize these: we used them to hang gates in fields well away from any power source!

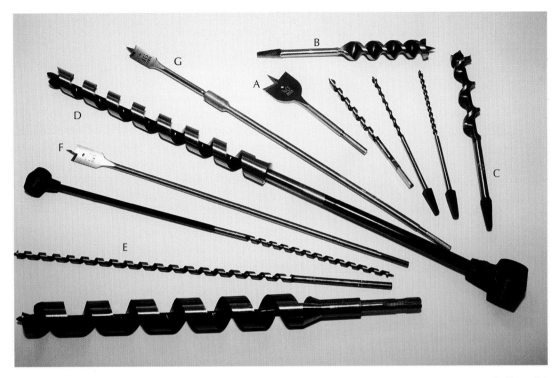

Fig. 51 A range of drill bits: a: flat; b: 'Jennings' pattern auger; c: solid centre auger; d: 'Scotch' screw-eyed; e: long multi-speed; f: long flat; g: flat with extension.

COUNTERSINK BITS

These are necessary when fitting screws, as they bore the recess to take the head (Fig. 53g). They come in a variety of shapes and sizes for use in hand or powered drills. A pilot hole is required as a guide so they can be centred on the screw.

DOWEL BITS

A simple 'twist' bit with spurs and a centre point (Figs. 52f and 53d); the spurs enable the bit to cut a much cleaner hole, and the point helps to stop it wandering off line.

ENGINEER'S BIT

The standard 'twist' bits found in most workshops (Fig. 52c): they have their uses when boring wood, but are really designed for metal cutting. They may be made from carbon steel or HSS; sometimes just the cutting edge is made from HSS. When using these bits it is advisable to punch the centre of the hole before you start to drill; unlike the dowel bits they can wander off line.

FLAT BITS

A very simple but useful bit, also known as a 'spade' bit (Figs. 51a and 51f): with a long lead point, these are excellent for drilling at an angle into the workface. They come in a range of sizes up to about 38mm, although I have seen some at about 50mm. Best results are obtained with a fairly fast drilling speed. Extension shanks are available (Fig. 51g) if deep

55

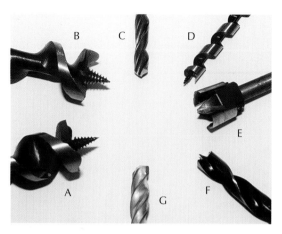

Fig. 52 Close-up of some drill bit tips: a: 'Jennings' auger; b: solid centre auger; c: engineer's; d: multi-speed; e: Forstner; f: dowel; g: masonry.

drilling is required. Take care with these as they are pretty vicious, and don't respect the exit face at all!

FORSTNER BITS

For really clean, shallow holes you won't beat a Forstner, or pattern maker's, bit (Figs. 52e and 53b): a range of these bits will always find a use in the workshop; they are ideal for fitting the round, recessed hinges you find on kitchen units. Take care when boring, as they can clog up quite quickly.

HOLE SAWS

A set of these is essential, in particular for work around the house (Fig. 53a). There are various types on the market but the operating principles are similar: a centrally fitted engineer or dowel bit locates and bores the middle, whilst a saw-toothed outer cutter removes the required diameter of waste. The central bit remains constant, but the outer saw-toothed bits can be changed, thus allowing different sized holes to be bored.

MASONRY AND PERCUSSION BITS

These bits are used for cutting stone or concrete, and will normally have a tungsten carbide tip, or TCT (Fig. 52g); this tip is necessarily very hard-wearing and has a long life. When using hammer drills it is best to use the specialist percussion bits – these will last longer because they are designed to take much more punishment. These are always a useful addition to any woodworker's tool kit.

MISCELLANEOUS

An endless variety of different drill bits will be found at sales of old tools. Most have been designed for a specific use and then been superseded by a more efficient style. Other craftsmen might swear by their 'saw-toothed' or 'spoon' bits and certainly they all have their place, but alternatives can be found. Some of the most useful gadgets are those that might help reduce the number of changes required to do a job. Combination bits that allow you to bore and then

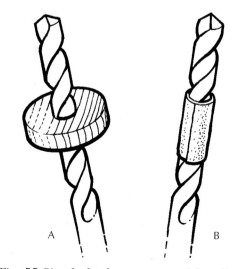

Fig. 55 Simple depth gauges: a: with a disc of wood or ply; b: with some tape.

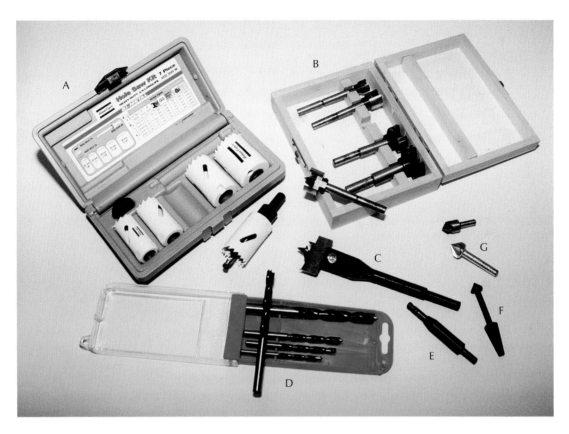

Fig. 53 Odds and ends: a: set of hole saws; b: range of Forstner bits; c: expansive bit; d: set of HSS engineer's bits; e: hinge pilot hole centre device; f: countersink bit for a brace; g: countersink bits for powered tools.

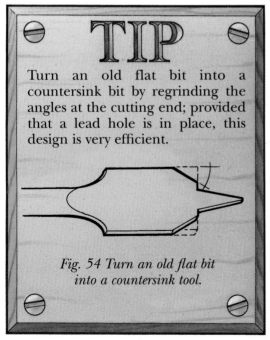

TIP

Turn an old flat bit into a countersink bit by regrinding the angles at the cutting end; provided that a lead hole is in place, this design is very efficient.

Fig. 54 Turn an old flat bit into a countersink tool.

countersink, or counter bore, all in one action are always useful. One of the best, in my opinion, is the gadget that allows you to bore centrally through a hinge hole (Fig. 53e); without this tool I always tend to go off centre. Depth gauges are another one for this group, though they can easily be home made (Fig. 55a and b). Plug cutters are also very useful, especially if your work requires a good surface finish. Always think through the likely amount of use you will get from any of these bits; if you can afford them, and if they will save time and effort, then add them to your box!

— 4 —

CUTTING AND PLANING

The tools in this chapter have also been hammer-graded on a scale from one to five – the least to the most essential, five hammers indicating the most practical to buy initially on a limited budget.

CHISELS

In many workshops chisels must take the most abuse! If we are honest, how many times have we reached for a chisel to open a tin of paint? I know I have. In fact I used to keep a couple of old, tatty chisels in my box for on-site work, specifically for those occasions when I wanted to use them for a job they weren't designed for – chasing out plaster and finishing off putty in windows used to be the classic ones; or even chopping through nails if no cold chisel was to hand! And chopping plaster with a good mortice chisel is bad news. Using a tatty one for this sort of job is just about acceptable – but whatever you do, don't pay a high price for top quality chisels and then abuse them.

My own collection of chisels is quite large, but I still haven't got one for every eventuality. I started with a couple of straight-edged chisels, then later bought a set of four 'Stanley' bevel-edged buttress chisels, and eventually the rest of the matching set. These chisels are primarily designed for paring, and cutting across, or partly across, the grain, although at the time I had to use them for all jobs, some of which might have been better served with a different type of chisel; however,

over the years I was able to afford better and more specifically designed chisels. And eventually I invested in a mortice machine, which has effectively done away with the need to cut mortice holes by hand – though not altogether: there are still those delicate and awkward jobs that need a hand-cut hole.

Basically there are two types of chisel blade: square-edged (Fig. 56a and 58b/c), and bevel-edged (Fig. 56b and 58a). Square-edged chisels are, very broadly, used for cutting straight holes (Fig. 59b), whilst bevel-edged are used to get into the angles of, say, dovetail joints (Fig. 59a); both are universally used for paring. Blades come in various sizes and shapes, and are discussed below under each of the chisels named. They are fitted to the handle in several ways: first, the older style

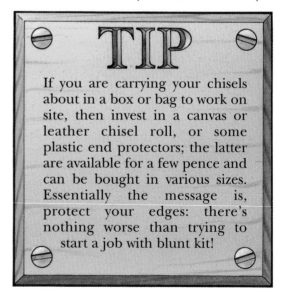

TIP

If you are carrying your chisels about in a box or bag to work on site, then invest in a canvas or leather chisel roll, or some plastic end protectors; the latter are available for a few pence and can be bought in various sizes. Essentially the message is, protect your edges: there's nothing worse than trying to start a job with blunt kit!

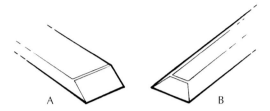

Fig. 56 Chisel shapes: a: square-edged;
b: bevel-edged.

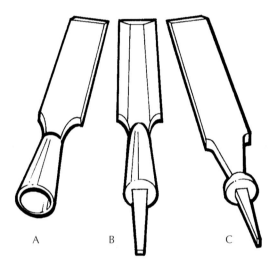

Fig. 57 How chisels are fitted to their handles:
a: socket; b: combined tang and buttress;
c: tang only.

'socket' fitting (Fig. 57a) has been largely
replaced with a combined 'tang' and
'buttressed' blade fitting (Fig. 57b);
modern plastic 'shatterproof' handles,
specially designed for hard wear, generally
use this construction (Fig. 60). Square-
edged chisel blades tend to be attached
using a 'tang' only (Fig. 57c); if the chisel
is to be used for cutting work with a
mallet, there is often a leather washer
between blade and handle to help absorb
shock. In addition there will probably be a
metal ferrule at the top of the handle to
prevent it splitting under impact. Paring

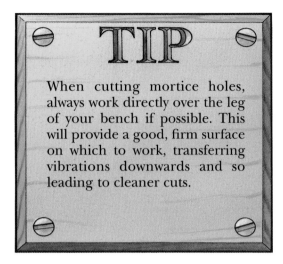

TIP

When cutting mortice holes,
always work directly over the leg
of your bench if possible. This
will provide a good, firm surface
on which to work, transferring
vibrations downwards and so
leading to cleaner cuts.

chisels that are used by hand will not have
this feature.

One of the most important features of any
chisel will be its ability to maintain its
cutting 'edge' for longish periods between
sharpening. Modern chisels tend to be
'drop forged' – that is, shaped between
two 'formers' when red hot (Fig. 60) – and
the steel used is most probably high
carbon or alloy steel, and it is generally
accepted that blades made in this way will
not hold their edge as long as those that
are hand forged. In the latter method the
blade is beaten into shape using many
blows, and it is this repetitive hammering,
I understand, that alters the structure and
characteristics of the steel to one that
keeps a better edge. In both methods of
blade construction they will need to be
'tempered', a process that involves
heating and cooling the finished blade in
a specific way. If the result is too brittle the
blade will keep an edge but chip easily; if
too soft, the edge is soon lost.

The modern drop-forged chisel is more
than adequate for most purposes. If,
however, you are to use chisels for
prolonged periods, then – subject to
available funds – you may like to seek out
new, top-of-the-range, hand-forged

Fig. 58 Close-up of some chisels: a: bevel-edged; b: narrow, square-edged mortice; c: wide, square-edged paring chisel.

chisels. A good source of second-hand chisels will be at local and national auctions and sales, where you might find that perfect chisel at a bargain price!

Handles are important. The best woods for those handles that are likely to be struck are those that are shock resistant, for instance hickory, beech, boxwood and ash. The shatterproof plastic handle can usually be struck with a hammer if you really have to, but I don't recommend it! And if they are to be used in hand work, then make sure there are no ridges or rough surfaces, as these lead to blisters. Wood is often used for the more traditional hand applications, when no sharp blows will be administered except by

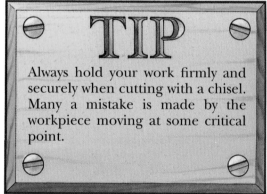

TIP

Always hold your work firmly and securely when cutting with a chisel. Many a mistake is made by the workpiece moving at some critical point.

the heel of the hand, so they should mould comfortably into your grip. Rosewood is popular, but most hardwoods will do; like the blade, the choice of handle style depends upon the work to be done.

The list of differing types of chisel below is not exhaustive. I have tried to allocate a common name to each one

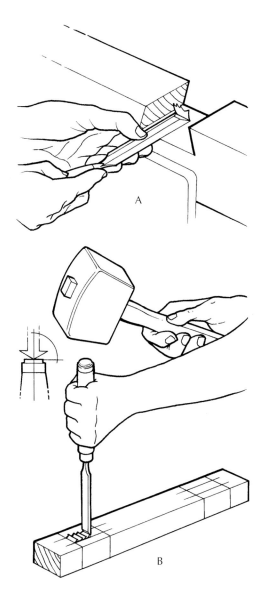

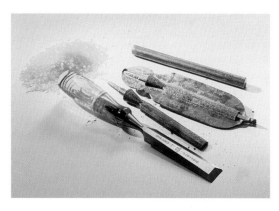

Fig. 60 How a modern impact-resistant plastic- or resin-handled chisel is constructed. (Record Hand Tools)

CORNER CHISELS

Of fairly simple design, these chisels are a specialist tool for cleaning up corners (Fig. 61a); as such they are not essential, but are certainly useful to have around, particularly with the increased use of routers for creating housing joints. A couple of quick taps and the corners are squared out.

CRANKED CHISELS

Fundamentally a paring chisel, these are used by hand to get into awkward places (Fig. 62c); they can be both square- and bevel-edged. This chisel comes into its own when cleaning out long housing joints across the grain, since the handle remains above the surface, thus allowing a much cleaner and flatter internal surface to be fashioned. They are one of the pattern maker's traditional tools, and as such are a specialist item.

Fig. 59 Different chisels for different jobs: a: the bevel-edged can reach into recesses and clean them out; b: the straight-edged can cut square holes.

described, but I dare say some readers may recognize a particular chisel under another name. There is also a certain amount of ambiguity today in both manufacture and name.

DRAWER LOCK CHISELS

Made entirely of steel, this little chisel is for cutting out drawer lock recesses (Fig. 61b); the cutting edges are set at right

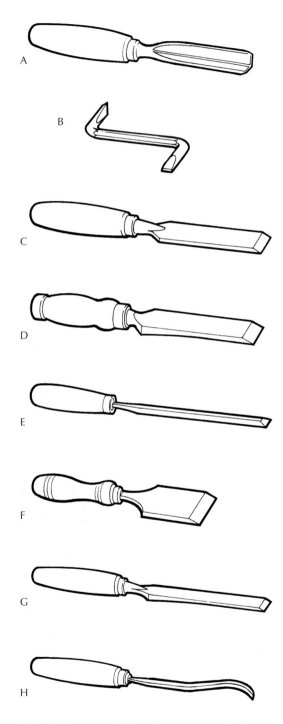

Fig. 61 A range of chisels: a: corner; b: drawer lock; c: register; d: mortice; e: bevel-edged paring; f: pocket or butt; g: sash; h: swan-neck.

angles to each other so that corners can be cut easily. The chisel is struck on the heel away from the cutting edge. Once more it is a specialist bit of kit: useful to have around, but not essential – unless, that is, you want to fit a lock to a drawer after it has been made!

FIRMER CHISELS

This is quite a desirable chisel; it derives its name from a thicker, thus firmer, square-edged blade. Often called a 'register' chisel, which was used by shipbuilders, it can be used as a universal tool for paring and light morticing (Figs. 61c and 62h). A set of these will cover a great deal of the general work carried out.

MORTICE CHISELS

These square-edged chisels are designed with a much greater thickness of blade to ensure they don't snap when used for heavy mortice work (Fig. 61d); this allows leverage to be exerted without worrying that the blade might break. There are many variations on this theme. Modern mortice chisels may be designed to look like a firmer chisel, but the body of the blade has been thickened out (Fig. 62g). If hand morticing is contemplated, three or four of these chisels will be most useful. Narrow versions of this are often called 'sash' chisels (Fig. 61g); the name comes from specialist use when cutting the narrow mortices in sash window bars.

PARING CHISELS

Generally these are bevel-edged tools, but not necessarily so. They come in a variety of lengths (Figs. 61e and 62a/b/d) and widths. I have a very old 50mm (2in)-wide square-edged one that I picked up for a few pence at a sale somewhere (Fig. 58c); used by hand, they need to have good

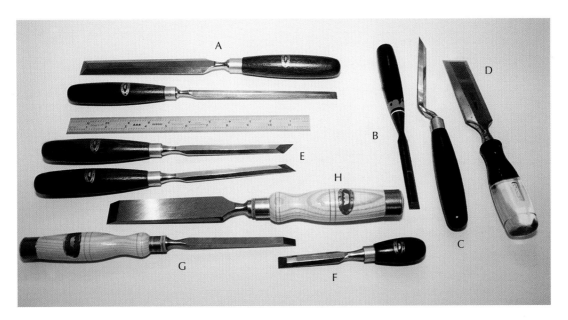

Fig. 62 Even more chisels! a: long paring; b: standard bevel-edged paring; c: cranked bevel-edged; d: wide paring; e: skew bevel-edged; f: butt; g: mortice; h: firmer.

balance and a comfortable handle for best control. Alongside the firmer I would recommend a full set of these for most workshops.

POCKET CHISELS

Called this because they are rarely longer than 225mm (9in) long; shorter ones are also known as 'butt' chisels (Figs. 61f and 62f). These are nice chisels to have around, the wider ones being particularly useful when fitting hinges. The width gives a bit more stability and produces a flatter surface onto which the hinge can be seated.

SKEW CHISELS

Also useful to have around, but not a necessity. They come in both square- and bevel-edged versions, and are usually 'handed' (Fig. 62e). The angle is generally set at 60 degrees, and is most useful for getting a clean cut on spiral and interlocked grain. The point, of course, is often used to get into tight corners that need cleaning out.

SWAN-NECK CHISELS

Sometimes called a 'lock-mortice' chisel, these are especially useful for cleaning out deep mortice holes, mostly created when trying to fit locks! Older versions will have a 'heel' (Fig. 61h) which aids leverage. Although they can generally be found in a limited range of widths, not many are used today.

I have deliberately omitted descriptions of two additional classes of chisel: gouges, used probably only occasionally by the general woodworker but essential nonetheless, as are other types of chisel, for wood carvers; and the Japanese chisel. This latter group is made with laminated steel blades, which keep an extremely good edge. The handles are fitted with a combination of socket and tang. If a lot of

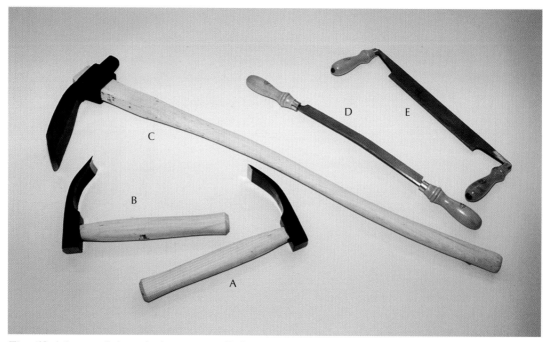

Fig. 63 Adzes and draw knives: a: small chisel-head adze; b: small gouge adze; c: large carpenter's adze; d: curved draw knife; e: straight draw knife.

hand work is anticipated, then these are certainly worth considering. However, they are not really suitable for amateur use due to the cost and care involved with looking after them.

her legs. The knack of doing this takes a while to learn: it is ideal for rough cutting 'green' or freshly felled wood, but not a tool to use on old dry stuff – that is hard work!

ADZES AND DRAW KNIVES

ADZES

These warrant a mention, but are unlikely to be found in the modern workshop. The large, long-handled carpenter's adze can have both straight (Fig. 63c) and curved cutting edges, and is traditionally used for squaring off large, round trunks of wood to make beams and, to a lesser degree, chair seat shaping. The user stands above the workpiece and chips away, swinging the adze back and forth between his or

Fig. 64 A simple 'shaving horse' for use with draw knives.

The smaller adzes for closer hand work usually have either a straight, chisel-type head (Fig. 63a), or a curved gouge-type head (Fig. 62b); both of these are still used by Windsor chair makers for shaping the seat. Some of the same principles apply as with the larger adze: the workpiece is straddled and the cuts are made from above, or the piece is held vertically in a vice and the cutting action is down. Most of the shaping of these seats will be made with cuts across the grain to avoid pieces splitting out along the grain.

DRAW KNIVES

Not essential tools for the workshop, draw knives echo a past era of woodworking. There are two basic styles: those with straight cutting blades (Fig. 63e), and those with curved cutting blades for hollowing (Fig. 63d). As the name suggests, the tool is grasped in both hands and drawn towards the user to achieve a cut. The workpiece is held firmly in a vice or, more traditionally, a 'shaving horse' (Fig. 64): in this case the user sits on the horse at one end, and the work is placed on the central block and locked into place when the feet push the swivelling frame forwards. The draw knife is most useful for roughing down squares and for simple chair work.

SAWS FOR CUTTING WOOD

The number of different types of saw that have been developed is truly astounding – and by this I mean the different types of saw made for specific tasks. I have several of these now, although I recall managing, many years ago, with just two: a 'ripsaw' made from an old wooden handle and a short chunk of bandsaw blade, and a 'tenon' saw. I still have the latter, though happily the old ripsaw has long gone – it was a terrible thing to use! It had a nasty cast to one side, caused by the original roll of steel, which made it very difficult to cut a straight line.

UNDERSTANDING TOOTH DESIGN

Before identifying the many different types of saw, it is important to explore the

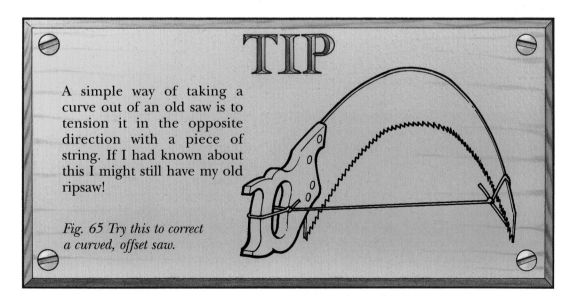

A simple way of taking a curve out of an old saw is to tension it in the opposite direction with a piece of string. If I had known about this I might still have my old ripsaw!

Fig. 65 Try this to correct a curved, offset saw.

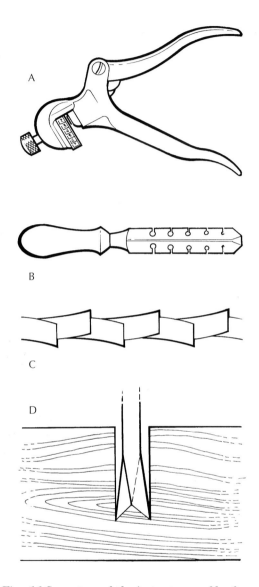

Fig. 66 Sawsets and the importance of kerf: a: a pre-set sawset; b: a hand set; c: plan view of a 'set' saw; d: set correctly, the 'kerf' will give clearance to the blade.

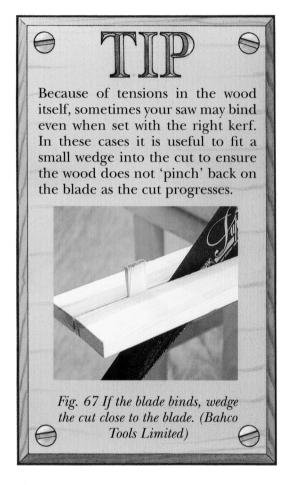

TIP

Because of tensions in the wood itself, sometimes your saw may bind even when set with the right kerf. In these cases it is useful to fit a small wedge into the cut to ensure the wood does not 'pinch' back on the blade as the cut progresses.

Fig. 67 If the blade binds, wedge the cut close to the blade. (Bahco Tools Limited)

way in which the specific saw type is made, and to understand how the tooth of a saw works. Generally saw teeth will be sharpened and then 'set' with a specialist bit of kit called a 'sawset': in this process, teeth are alternately set – or bent, putting it crudely – to one side or the other of the saw blade. Accurate sawsets are like a pair of pliers, although simpler ones are also effective (Figs. 66a, b and c). The objective of the set is to provide clearance on each side of the saw blade to allow it to cut without binding (Fig. 66d).

The combined width of cut made by these alternately set teeth is called the 'kerf' (Fig. 66d) and it is determined by several factors, one of which is the thickness of the steel in the saw blade, and another the type of work it will do. As regards the latter, when working with wet wood, for instance, a wider kerf is helpful as wet fibres tend to spring back and bind on the saw blade. However, two further factors should be taken into consideration

Cutting thin plywood can be a nightmare, as it will flop around and, more often than not, pinch on the saw blade. To help make life easier, make sure the ply is fully supported and then lift the cut piece slightly as you progress down the sheet.

Fig. 68 With light materials, lifting the edge makes sawing easier. (Bahco Tools Limited)

when deciding upon the amount of kerf: firstly, a wide kerf produces more waste, and secondly, removing this waste takes more effort. The kerf should be just enough to allow the saw blade to work efficiently.

WHICH SAW TO USE

Tooth design is of paramount importance when considering which saw to use for what job. Traditionally there are two basic types: those for cutting down the grain,

and those for cutting across the grain (Figs. 69a and c); in each case the teeth will be sharpened to give a slightly different cutting profile (Figs. 69b and d). For example, the ripsaw works with the grain and cuts on the forward stroke; wood adjacent to the cut on the top surface does not break out very much, but

Fig. 69 Different saws for different jobs: a: ripsaw teeth for cutting down the grain; b: the ripsaw cut; c: the crosscut saws across the grain; d: the crosscut.

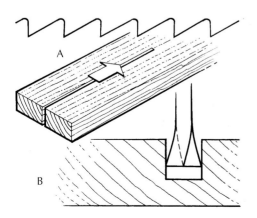

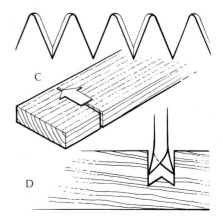

can on the underside. This is because the crosscut tooth is designed to cut the fibres before any waste is removed; hopefully this results in a nice clean cut on the top surface, but inevitably there will be some breakout, or 'spelshing' as it is called, on the underside. These days tooth technology has moved on to include 'universal' designs that can cut both down and across the grain. These saws are excellent value for money. However, I would recommend that for cutting joints it is still best to use the saw that is designed for the job.

The size of the tooth itself is also important (Fig. 71). Thus big teeth will remove a lot of waste and should therefore cut quickly, and are ideal for those rough carcasing jobs, or where the surface finish is not too important. Smaller teeth will produce less waste and a finer cut, just right for such jobs as jointing. Teeth numbers are classified by how many there are per inch of saw blade – teeth per inch, or tpi as a general abbreviation. For heavy ripsaw work and some occasional rough crosscutting, something between 3.5–6 tpi will be sufficient; for crosscutting and general panel work about 6–10 tpi; for

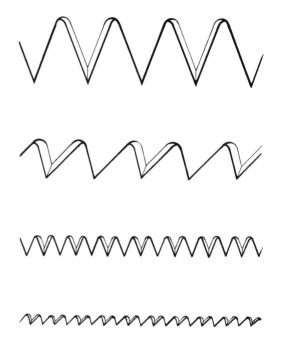

Fig. 71 A range of different-sized saw teeth.

cutting tenon joints and for clean panel work 10–14 tpi, when a much finer cut is required; and for fine veneer, cabinet and model work, 14–18 tpi will give excellent results.

TIP

If the underside surface finish is as important as the topside, then provide some support during cutting; a bit of waste placed underneath will be sufficient.

Fig. 70 Use a bit of gash stock underneath to help prevent break-out. (Bahco Tools Limited)

HARDPOINT SAWS

Traditional saws will be made from steel that allows the teeth to be resharpened; we will discuss this later. However, many manufacturers now produce saws with hardened tips to the teeth, generally called 'hardpoint' saws. Their one obvious disadvantage is that they can't be resharpened, however they do have several advantages – probably most important is their relatively low cost, in that most hardpoint saws are mass produced. This, and the fact that they are designed to be disposable (because you can't sharpen them) also means they are less likely to be pinched.

The hardpoint saw stays sharp for much longer than a traditional one – up to five times as long, or even more, some claim. The hardness also allows for a certain amount of abuse in that the teeth don't have to be protected from knocks so much. These saws are especially useful when cutting modern particleboards such as medium density fibreboard (MDF) and chipboard, as both of these contain resins that quickly blunt a traditional saw.

There is a truly huge range of hardpoint saws, and several factors should be borne in mind when buying. For instance, the fine-tuning of tooth design will give better performance, or so the manufacturers claim – though we have to be swayed by their extensive knowledge and testing facilities, and take most of this on trust. Perhaps most important is to consider the type of work you want to do with the saw, and then try and match it to a particular manufacturer's design. Look for additional features, too: some models incorporate handles that will help with rough marking out – they have shoulders set at various angles. Non-stick, therefore non-bind, coatings are also popular. Anything that makes the sawing process

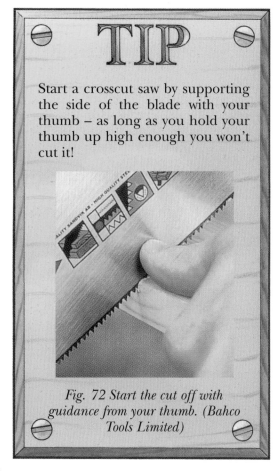

TIP

Start a crosscut saw by supporting the side of the blade with your thumb – as long as you hold your thumb up high enough you won't cut it!

Fig. 72 Start the cut off with guidance from your thumb. (Bahco Tools Limited)

easier and more accurate should be considered.

SAW LENGTH

The length of your saws for different jobs is important. Long-stroke ripsawing is ideally achieved with saws that are 24–28in (610–710mm) long. Crosscutting does not need such a long stroke, so a saw 22–24in (560–610mm) is ideal. Panel saws are slightly shorter at about 20–22in (510–560mm). Jointing saws tend to be anything from 4–18in (100–455mm). If you don't want, or can't afford to have, a saw for every eventuality, then choose two or three to cover your needs.

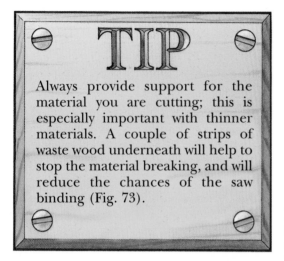

TIP

Always provide support for the material you are cutting; this is especially important with thinner materials. A couple of strips of waste wood underneath will help to stop the material breaking, and will reduce the chances of the saw binding (Fig. 73).

panel saws: these are made from flat, tempered steel with a longish, flexible blade that is generally tapered, and with traditional or hardpoint teeth. In the second category are the 'back' saws, where the blades tend to be shorter, thinner and of uniform width; they are used for accurate cutting, close to the mark, and produce little waste. To help control, the saw blade needs to be fairly rigid, and to

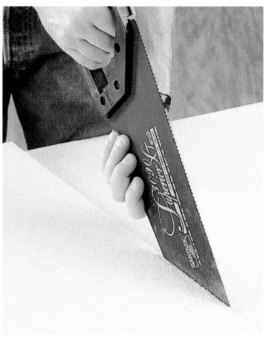

Fig. 74 For some of those long reach cuts, reverse the saw. (Bahco Tools Limited)

Fig. 73 When cutting thin materials they may need support underneath. (Bahco Tools Limited)

HANDSAWS

There are three main types of handsaw, with many variations. In the first category come the ripsaw, and the crosscut and

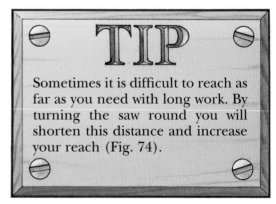

TIP

Sometimes it is difficult to reach as far as you need with long work. By turning the saw round you will shorten this distance and increase your reach (Fig. 74).

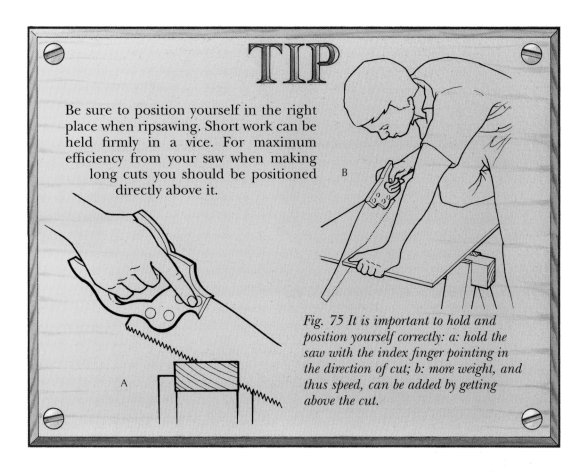

TIP

Be sure to position yourself in the right place when ripsawing. Short work can be held firmly in a vice. For maximum efficiency from your saw when making long cuts you should be positioned directly above it.

B

A

Fig. 75 It is important to hold and position yourself correctly: a: hold the saw with the index finger pointing in the direction of cut; b: more weight, and thus speed, can be added by getting above the cut.

achieve this a brass or metal back is fitted. In the final category is the 'framesaw': these can come with a large frame and a fairly wide blade for ripping and crosscutting; smaller ones tend to have a thin, narrow blade for curved work. In both cases the blade is tensioned between the two ends of the frame; keeping the blade taught means that it will cut in the desired direction.

JAPANESE SAWS

There is another group of saws that particularly warrants a mention. As we become more internationalized, design technology transfers become much easier, and in recent years we have seen an increase in the number of 'Japanese' saws available in our shops. From a Northern Hemisphere point of view these saws have teeth the wrong way round, so that instead of the cut being made away from you, it is made towards you; this action is called 'pull' sawing. The advantages of these types of saw come from this reverse action. Thus, traditional backsaws have a thin blade that has to be strengthened to achieve the forward cut, whereas the pull saw can be made from steel that is just as thin or even thinner, and without any need for strengthening. With their specialist tooth design they are very easy to control, and only remove a small amount of waste. These saws are becoming very popular and should be given due consideration when deciding what to buy.

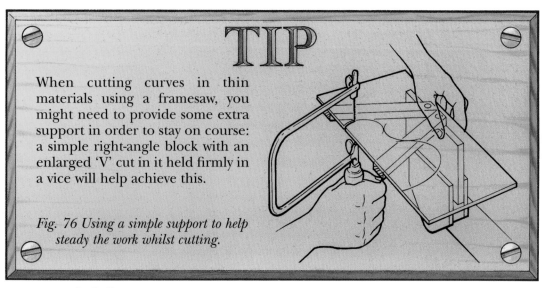

When cutting curves in thin materials using a framesaw, you might need to provide some extra support in order to stay on course: a simple right-angle block with an enlarged 'V' cut in it held firmly in a vice will help achieve this.

Fig. 76 Using a simple support to help steady the work whilst cutting.

RIPSAW

The details of the ripsaw have been discussed above. If you are likely to cut a lot of timber without mechanical aid, then one of these is essential: so buy a good one and look after it (Fig. 77c).

CROSSCUT AND PANEL SAWS

Although recognized as two different types of saw, you might find it useful to try and combine these two to avoid having too many. The specification of these saws has also been discussed; however for general use, one about 22in (560mm) long, with 8 or 10 tpi should be sufficient.

HARDPOINT SAWS

There are so many of these available that they warrant a book of their own! Looking through one of the major manufacturer's catalogues I note they make a hardpoint for most of the regular types of saw. Remember they should be cheap and sharp, and thrown away when

blunt. For general use a 'universal' is probably best (Fig. 77b): this is 20in (560mm) long, with 8 tpi. It is ideal for cutting laminates and chipboard, and also down and across the grain of solid wood.

TENON SAW

Always have one of these in your kit bag. They come in a variety of shapes and sizes: the one illustrated is12in (300mm) long, with a brass back and 13 tpi (Fig. 77a). For

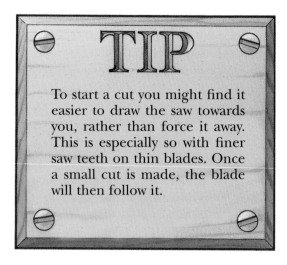

To start a cut you might find it easier to draw the saw towards you, rather than force it away. This is especially so with finer saw teeth on thin blades. Once a small cut is made, the blade will then follow it.

Fig. 77 Some saws: a: backed tenon saw; b: universal hardpoint saw; c: traditional top quality ripsaw.

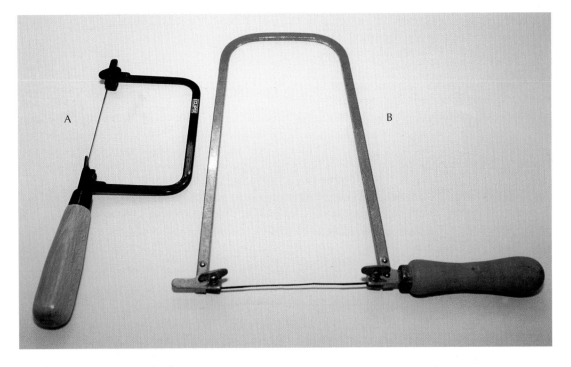

Fig. 79 a: Coping saw; b: fretsaw.

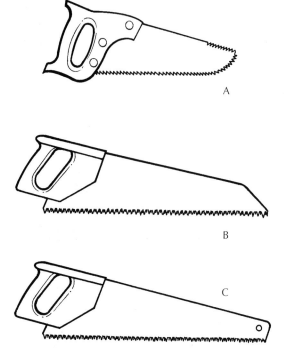

Fig. 78 More saws: a: floorboard saw, with a rounded cutting edge to start the cut off; b: short wallboard saw; c: toolbox saw.

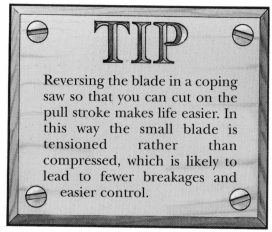

long shoulder work, a saw up to 18in (450mm) long is not unusual. Start with a 10 or 12in (280 or 300mm), and buy a longer one later if you need to and can afford it.

FLOORBOARD SAW

This is just one of various specialist saws that are available (Fig. 78a), designed to help those who wish to gain access to underfloor installations. This one has a rounded cutting edge to start penetration. Once through, the saw is turned over and the short, straight edge used until a wide enough cut is made to take the whole of the blade. A useful saw when you need one, they are generally about 12in (300mm) long, with fairly coarse teeth at about 8 or10 tpi.

WALLBOARD SAW

Another specialist saw designed to penetrate and then cut wallboard materials (Fig 78b). It is a short saw, 15in (380mm) or so long, that is very useful for getting into awkward spaces. It has fairly coarse teeth at about 8 to 10 tpi. Not a lot of use in the workshop, but handy for site work.

SHORT OR TOOLBOX SAWS

These can be bought specifically to fit into a toolbox (Fig. 78c), and are about the same size and configuration as the wallboard saw. They are handy to have in your site-work toolbox. An old ripsaw or crosscut saw hacked off to create a shorter one will probably be just as useful, if you have a spare one.

COPING SAW

This is the smallest of the framesaws (Fig. 79a): the 6in (150mm) or so frame is generally made to allow about a 5in (125mm) depth of cut. The blade is tensioned between the two ends of the frame, and tightened by turning the handle; it will have 14–18 tpi. The blade can be turned in the frame, quite simply, to allow for shaped and side cutting. Holes can be cut in the centre of a workpiece. Drill a hole big enough to take the blade, dismantle the saw, thread the blade through the hole, reassemble the saw and start to cut. A useful saw to have around the workshop.

FRETSAW

Very similar to the coping saw, although this design has been around for much longer (Fig. 79b). Normally with an increased number of tpi, up to 32, it can perform much as a coping saw, with the

added advantage of a deeper frame; cuts up to 12in (300mm) deep can be made, providing the frame is big enough. It is ideal for really fine work, but not for cutting through solid chunks of wood!

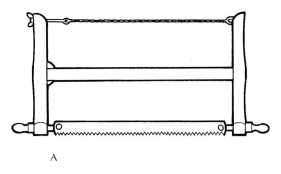

A

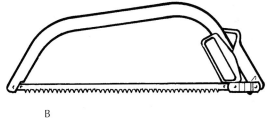

B

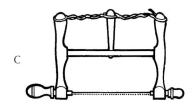

C

Fig. 81 Bowsaws: a: long traditional; b: large modern; c: small bench.

BOWSAWS

There are several types of bowsaw. The traditional, long bowsaw (Fig. 81a) is about 30in (760mm) in length, and generally made with a wooden frame; the blade is about 1in (25mm) wide, and is tensioned by tightening a cord or wire at

TIP

These smaller framesaws should be gripped firmly in both hands to help guide them. Do not exert too much pressure during the process, or try to cut very thick material.

Fig. 80 How to hold a small framesaw correctly.

Fig. 82 Even more saws: a: backed pull saw; b: backed dovetail; c: large veneer saw, with starting teeth on the top, and rounded edge; d: fast-cutting pull saw.

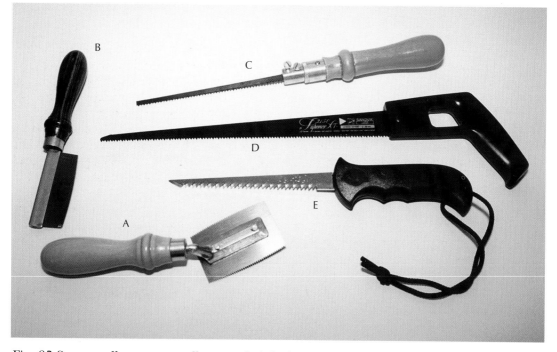

Fig. 83 Some small saws: a: small veneer; b: inlaying; c: pad; d: compass; e: small plasterboard.

the top – the two end frames pivot on a central rail, thus tightening the blade. It can be used for ripsawing and crosscut sawing. Like the other framesaws, the blade can be turned to aid sawing direction. The long bowsaw is not often seen in workshops today, having been superseded by other saws.

The modern, large metal-framed bowsaw (Fig. 81b) is available in a variety of lengths from 18in to 4ft (450mm to 1,220mm). This is not a replacement for the old bowsaw above, as it has a different function: it is designed for cutting logs. The tooth shape allows for cut in both directions, and the blade is tensioned across the gap between the two ends. If you have a lot of really rough sawing to do, one of these might be useful. I find them difficult to control for anything other than cutting firewood!

The third type of bowsaw is probably about halfway in size between the two above and the coping saw and fretsaw (Fig. 81c). The same basic principles apply, in that the blade is tensioned between the two ends: in this case a cord is twisted, pivoting the frame on the centre rail, and locked off with a flat toggle stick. Frames will vary in size from 10 or 12in to 16 or 18in (250–450mm). A variety of blades are available, though one about ¼in (6mm) wide will probably suit best. It is a coarse-cutting saw of about 10 tpi. Quite a handy saw to have, but don't expect to wear it out!

DOVETAIL SAW

As the name suggests, this is a backsaw specifically designed for cutting dovetails (Fig. 82b). Saws like this are usually 8–9in (200–230mm) long, and will have a thin blade supported by the back, with little set and about 18–20 tpi. Kept sharp and tidy, they are invaluable if you have a great deal of hand jointing to do.

PULL SAWS

We have already discussed this type of saw. Suffice it to say that for every push-saw type there will be its equivalent as a pull saw, and they come in various shapes and sizes: the two illustrated (Fig. 82) are both 'Westernized' and come with removable handles. The full backsaw (Fig. 82a) is the equivalent of the tenon and dovetail saws: about 11in (280mm) long, with 15 tpi, and the tooth and blade design is such that it provides a very fine cut for detailed work. Other similar saws are available with finer teeth configuration for veneer work.

The second, larger saw (Fig. 82d) is about 15in (380mm) long; this one is a fast-cutting, general-purpose saw with 8–10 tpi. As a starting point you could do worse than buy a couple of saws like these. However, if you decide to set up your workshop entirely with pull saws, then buy the best you can afford.

VENEER SAW

The large saw illustrated is often called a veneer saw (Fig. 82c), but inappropriately, and in this classification is rather out of place. The rounded, cutting top edge is designed to help with a penetration cut in the middle of thin sheet materials. It is about 12in (300mm) long, with about 12 tpi. It is ideal for the job it has been designed for, but not for fine work with thin veneers.

The short, small saw illustrated (Fig. 83a) is more appropriately called a veneer saw since it is designed specifically for cutting fine, thin veneers with precision. With little or no set, and with 15–18 tpi, the saw can be used against a straight edge; when blunt, the blade is reversed. With the additional benefit of the cranked handle, these saws can often be used for flush cutting.

Fig. 84 Handy saws: a: large gent's; b: small gent's; c: large reversible; d: small reversible; e: double-sided flush-cutting; f: single-sided flush-cutting.

INLAYING SAW

This is a small, purpose-made saw (Fig. 83b) about 3in (75mm) long, with a brass back to provide rigidity. With about 20 tpi, it can slice very thin strips of veneer or wood into pieces of inlay. This is an ideal saw for fine cabinetwork.

COMPASS SAW

These saws are specifically designed for cutting curves; the one illustrated (Fig. 83d) has a non-stick coating. With a fixed blade of about 12in (300mm), and about 10 tpi, the compass saw is one of a family that is used to cut holes and shapes away from the edge. A hole is drilled first and the saw inserted – though small diameter holes are not possible because of the width of the blade.

PADSAW

Another of the hole cutters, this saw is also known as a 'keyhole' saw. It is slightly different from the compass saw in that the blade can be extended or retracted, when it is not in use, within the handle (Fig. 83c). This feature also means that the extent to which the blade projects can be adjusted to suit thick or thin materials. For example when cutting thin materials a shorter stroke is best, and less likely to bend the blade. It is available in about the same basic sizes as a compass saw. The padsaw can cope with cutting solid wood up to 2in (50m) thick – though not without effort!

PLASTERBOARD SAW

This small saw is specifically designed for penetrating plasterboard (Fig. 83e), having a sharpened tip that can be forced through the plasterboard and jiggled around until the cut can start. A handy tool for this kind of work, but with limited application only.

GENT'S SAW

The name is a shortened version of 'gentleman's' saw. I understand they were first made in the 1800s for gentlemen hobbyists, rather than for trade or craftsmen. Unlike the small dovetail saws that traditionally have an open or closed 'pistol-grip' handle, the gent's saw was designed with a turned one. They come in various sizes, from 4–10in (100–250mm) long; the two illustrated are typical (Fig. 84a and b), the small one with 25 tpi and the larger 17 tpi. Similar tools will be found under various names such as 'model maker's' or 'jeweller's' saws. Like gent's saws, they are a useful addition to any toolbox for fine work.

REVERSIBLE SAW

Similar to the gent's saw, these have a cranked handle to allow access into difficult places from both sides. They come in many shapes and sizes, and are from 4–10in (100–250mm) long (Fig. 84c and d). Specifically designed with a high tpi – 15 to 20 is typical – they can be used for flush-cutting protruding dowels and wedges. Unscrewing one spring-loaded knurled nut allows the blade to be swung round and used from a different side. These really are a useful addition to any toolbox.

FLUSH-CUTTING SAWS

Of all the small, specialist saws, these must be amongst the most useful. They come in a variety of shapes and sizes (Fig. 84e and f) and are designed with a very thin blade

that is sharpened, and set to one side only. This feature allows dowels, plugs and wedges to be cut off flush with the surface from which they protrude; used carefully, a good, clean cut can be made that requires little finishing. They are not expensive; I use an old, tatty one for rough work, and a newer one for tidy work. Do not, however, use on finished facework unless you are very careful: I have found they always mark, no matter how careful you are.

METAL-CUTTING SAWS

A hacksaw is a useful item of kit to have in the workshop, for cutting off the occasional errant nail or screw – and there is a huge choice available.

FRAME HACKSAWS

The standard frame hacksaw (Fig. 85a) can take various lengths of blade, however a blade about 12in (300mm) long is usual; once located on the pins at each end, it can be tensioned by tightening the wing nut. If necessary it can be reversed to turn the whole thing into a pull saw. In addition to this, the blades can be turned round in the frame to cut to the left or right. I would thoroughly recommend one of these for most workshops.

GENERAL PURPOSE SAW

This saw (Fig. 85b) can take a blade for cutting metal or wood; it is ideal for cutting metal sheets or metal-faced sheet materials. A useful feature is that the handle can be angled at a variety of positions to suit any cutting direction. However, insofar as this saw is non-specific, in my opinion it is not an essential item for the workshop.

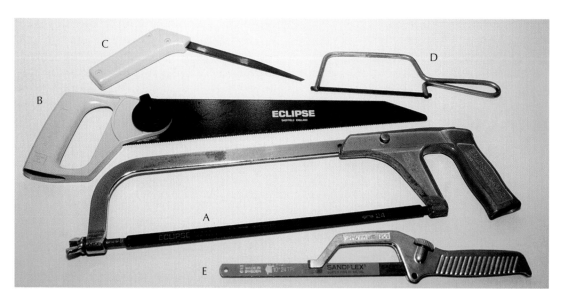

Fig. 85 Metal-cutting saws: a: frame hacksaw; b: general purpose; c: padsaw; d: junior hacksaw; e: mini hacksaw.

PADSAWS

Some padsaws (Fig. 85c) have a handle that can be adjusted to two different angles, a helpful feature if you are working in a tight place. They usually have universal blades, for cutting both wood and metal. Once again, a useful saw, but not essential.

JUNIOR HACKSAW

A smaller version of its big brother (Fig. 85d), and useful for those small metal-cutting jobs. Usually about 6in (150mm) long, it is a convenient tool to carry about in a box or bag. The frames are sprung: to release the blade, press the far end against something firm. Certainly a good choice for most toolboxes.

MINI HACKSAW

The mini hacksaw (Fig. 85e) possibly rates slightly better than the junior because it uses a standard hacksaw blade; this slots into the handle and is held in place with a thumbnut. Some extra support is provided from above to help prevent bending or breaking the blade.

ELECTRIC SAWS

Technology, manufacture and design have moved on since I was a boy; I only wish it had been more readily available then! Cutting up logs for firewood was a hated task, when my elder brother and I used to take it in turns with our father on one end of a large, double-handled crosscut saw (Fig. 86). These saws are anything from 4ft to 7ft (1,200–2,100mm) long, and they are a true 'pull' saw – they cut when you pull back on them, and there's a black art in getting them to cut straight. We spent hours sawing through large old beech trees, though perhaps this was character building – particularly when I later found out that a chainsaw could have done the job in less than half the time.

At fifteen I started work in a sawmill, and came across my first couple of

Fig. 86 A traditional double-sided crosscut saw.

electric power saws. One was a huge chainsaw. With a bar at well over 7ft (2,100mm), it took two or three of us to manoeuvre it about. Run by three phase, you would prop it up against a large trunk or pack of timber and set it going: if you were lucky, the weight of the bar would gradually take the cut down through the wood; if not, you had to hang on to the end opposite the motor by a handle. Slow and dirty, it was extremely efficient and quiet.

The other was a deadly, hand-held circular saw, definitely with a will of its own. With something like a 10in (250mm) blade, you would start a cut –and before you knew it, it would take off in a completely different direction. This could have been operator trouble, or something to do with the set on the teeth, I'm not sure – but whatever it was, you had to hang

on, letting go of the power trigger, until you came to a stop. Another little trick it had was to 'kick back' when you least expected it: you'd be making steady, straight progress, and then, towards the end of the cut, the whole thing would bind in the groove and nearly wrench your arm off as it kicked back.

In spite of these early experiences, and because I prefer sawing with as little effort as possible, I have become a power saw enthusiast and collected a range of kit. I depend most on my large, stand-alone bandsaw (see my book Small Bandsaw Techniques), closely followed by the other stand-alones: a pull-over crosscut and ripsaw. These three accomplish most of my sawing work, apart from fine handwork. I also have a couple of jigsaws and hand-held portable circular saws, though the latter are only used as a last resort against the 'big kit' already mentioned.

The power saws described here cannot replace the functions of all the different handsaws, but they will speed up the sawing process considerably.

SABRE SAW

This is a bigger version of the jigsaw (Fig. 87a); a reciprocating saw, it runs back and forth on a cam mechanism that mimics a sawing action. First the small shoe is placed against the workpiece, and then the cutting action can commence. Blades come in a variety of shapes and sizes, from 6–12in (150–300mm) long. Speed is measured by 'strokes per minute' and will probably provide a variable range from 0–2,400 in most cases.

The sabre saw has a variety of uses with blades to match. Probably best suited to site work, it can cut metal, wood and plastic with the appropriate blade fitted. The pistol grip, with power and speed controls, is gripped in one hand, and the other wraps round the fore-end part of the body to give direction and control the cut. Some blades are designed to pierce materials without the need of a starting hole.

Look out for the following when buying: first, a 'soft start' feature is useful – this means that as pressure is applied to the power on the trigger there won't be a sudden surge that might cause the blade to move or slip. Most will have pivoting shoes, but look to see if they have any other features that might lengthen blade life. And check the wattage: you should be expecting to do a lot of heavy work with one of these, and you will need the power.

I do not consider a saw like this to be essential, unless I had a specific, constant use for it.

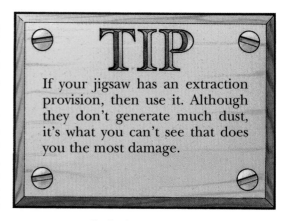

If your jigsaw has an extraction provision, then use it. Although they don't generate much dust, it's what you can't see that does you the most damage.

JIGSAWS

Probably one of the most versatile power tools you can have in the workshop: basically it is a power-driven padsaw or compass saw (Figs. 87b and c). If you drill a starting hole, internal curves and circles can be cut, and it

Fig. 87 Some powered saws: a: sabre; b: cordless jigsaw; c: jigsaw; d: alligator.

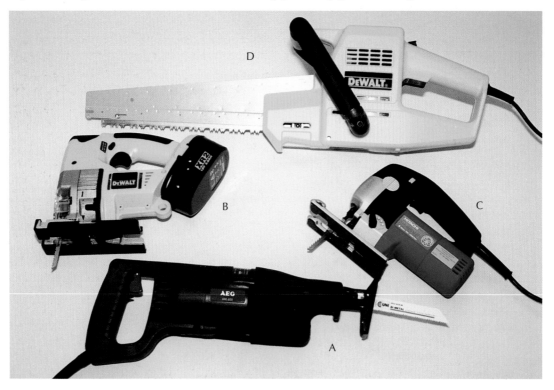

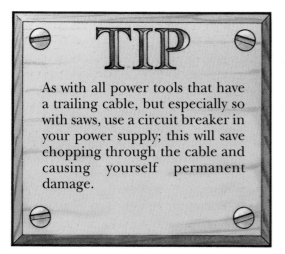

TIP

As with all power tools that have a trailing cable, but especially so with saws, use a circuit breaker in your power supply; this will save chopping through the cable and causing yourself permanent damage.

is also very useful for rounding and straight cutting. It will take sawing blades 2–5in (50–125mm) long, depending upon the materials to be cut, and some have an additional knife-blade feature for cutting foam and suchlike; these blades can be up to 6in (150mm) long. Others are sturdy enough to take a special rasp blade for shaping work. Unfortunately I seem unable to get the best out of a jigsaw – however hard I try, I can't keep it cutting in a straight line. Nevertheless, I still believe the jigsaw is a great bit of kit in the right hands!

Consider the following features when buying: first power, which as usual is based on wattage. The size of the motor will be dictated by the amount of running time and use that you will put the saw to; thus for long spells of continuous cutting you will need a motor of reasonable size, say around 500 or 600 watts, or more. For lighter, less continuous use a smaller motor will probably cope. Speeds are described as 'cut' or 'stroke' rates per minute, and variable speeds, some with soft starts, are common. It is helpful to be able to control the speed of cut as you go along. Remember, power is not the only criterion: build quality is also important, so be sure to look at the way the tool is put together. Those with part-metal bodies will probably cost more, but may be repairable if they go wrong. The base plate should be well finished to give a smooth ride. Most will angle up to 45 degrees in both directions, and if they can't, this should be reflected in the price.

Look at how the blades are fitted, because there are a few patented fast changeover systems available that do save time. All will have some sort of roller-

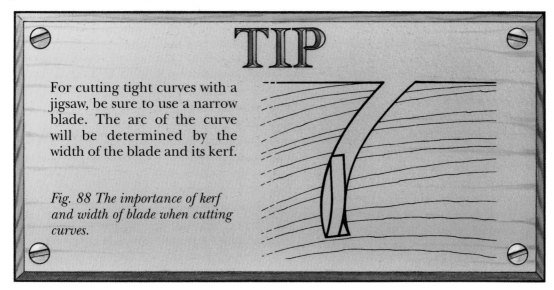

For cutting tight curves with a jigsaw, be sure to use a narrow blade. The arc of the curve will be determined by the width of the blade and its kerf.

Fig. 88 The importance of kerf and width of blade when cutting curves.

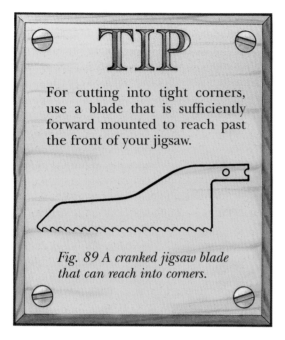

Fig. 89 A cranked jigsaw blade that can reach into corners.

TIP

For cutting into tight corners, use a blade that is sufficiently forward mounted to reach past the front of your jigsaw.

bearing support system for the blade, to reduce friction – and be wary of any that don't. A few jigsaws are fitted with a scrolling facility: this allows you to turn the blade slightly whilst cutting, useful for intricate work. An additional feature may be a pendulum action that allows the blade to swing forwards and backwards in the cutting cycle, thus taking out a bigger bite; coupled with the stroke rate, this determines how quickly you can, or should be able to cut. With softer materials a faster, bigger bite action will speed things up; conversely with harder, denser materials these high settings will probably lead to disaster! Metal, of course, should be cut on the slowest settings.

Length of cut will be determined by the power of your saw, the material being cut, and the blade used. There is a huge range of blades available, with each manufacturer claiming that theirs are the best. A very broad classification might be that the blades with big teeth are for softwoods, medium teeth are for hardwoods, and fine for metals; but read what the manufacturer states on the packaging. In addition to the usual materials, you can also cut, with the appropriate blade, ceramics, glass, stone, rubber, leather and many other things. One manufacturer I know of makes a table accessory into which the saw can be fitted; the table is then inverted and clamped to a bench so that the blade protrudes upwards. A fence attachment allows two-handed control of the workpiece for straight cutting, or when removed, curved cutting. If you have one of these, do use a 'push stick', and keep your fingers well out of the way of the blade!

The jigsaw has become even more versatile of late. The advances in battery technology have brought as many improvements to jigsaws (Fig. 87b) as they have to electric drills (see Chapter 3), and for the tradesman this has got to be useful when working on site, with no cables to lay out or cut through! For example, up on a roof the saw can be easily manoeuvred, and then placed safely to one side when not in use.

All in all, the jigsaw should be given serious consideration as a worthy tool for anyone's workshop or toolbox.

ALLIGATOR SAW

This is basically a powered handsaw for general purpose use (Fig. 87d), and most have been improved over the years to become quality bits of kit. They are primarily designed for the tradesman, and are invaluable when working on site, being nowhere near as dangerous or inaccurate as a chainsaw, yet more versatile than a jigsaw or a circular saw. They all work in a similar, basic fashion whereby two saw blades are attached to a protruding spine, back to back, and are connected to reciprocating drives that alternate the action of each opposing

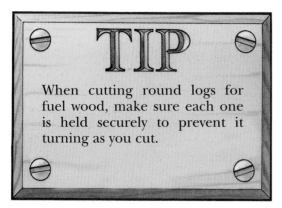

When cutting round logs for fuel wood, make sure each one is held securely to prevent it turning as you cut.

blade. The principle is as follows: put your hands palms flat together, and point them away from you; imagine that the bottom edge of each hand has saw teeth, and then rub them against each other back and forth. The spine holds the saw blades firmly in place, which allows for much more accurate cutting. A fair bit of waste is removed during the cutting action because the kerf is relatively wide to allow for spine clearance and the design of the teeth, which cut both ways.

One useful feature to look out for is a plunge action that allows you to start a cut without a hole; this will depend upon the blade configuration and spine design, so check this when buying. Overall blade length will probably range from 10–14in (250–350mm). Like a chainsaw, working round the object being cut can increase the depth of cut. If buying new, look at the blade changeover system: most will have some form of additional tool to do this, but some are less of a fiddle than others. Blades come in various shapes and sizes, to cut a wide variety of materials. Some hardened blades will cut through the softer thermal insulation building blocks, making them even more useful on a building site.

The alligator saw is not the most beautiful of tools, and it needs to be handled with respect; however, in my opinion it is preferable to a chainsaw.

Certainly if you are working on site, or with other outside construction work, you could do worse than have one of these. For the workshop, however, they are not essential.

CIRCULAR SAWS

A portable circular saw is a most convenient tool to have in the workshop, particularly if available space is limited, and you can't afford to buy a stand-alone machine. These saws are also benefitting from the advances in battery technology, and are now readily available with or without power cords (Figs. 90a and b). All you need to consider, when choosing, is what the saw will be used for.

With these saws, the depth of cut is the critical factor. I have come across some with a cutting depth capacity of up to 4in (100mm) or more, but the power needed to drive a blade that size makes the whole saw unwieldy – as the blade size increases, so does the size of motor required to drive it, and thus the size of the overall saw. Most modern saws will have a maximum capacity of just over 3⅜in (80–85mm), and motor sizes will start at 400–500 watts and go up to about 2,000 for the more industrial-type saws with bigger blades. The lighter-weight, cordless saw illustrated

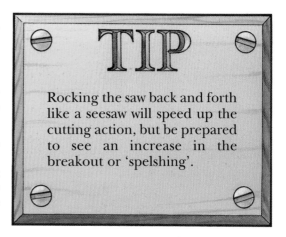

Rocking the saw back and forth like a seesaw will speed up the cutting action, but be prepared to see an increase in the breakout or 'spelshing'.

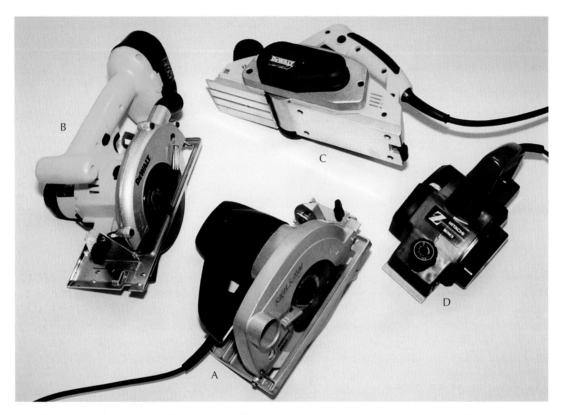

Fig. 90 Powered saws and planes: a: cordless circular; b: portable circular; c: medium-sized powered hand plane; d: lightweight powered hand plane.

(Fig. 90b) has a depth capacity of about 1 ½in (40mm) – not at all bad for this bit of kit!

By adjusting the sole plate, all these saws should be able to cut at angles up to 45 degrees, and then be returned to the

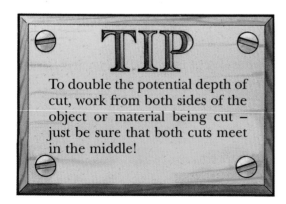

TIP

To double the potential depth of cut, work from both sides of the object or material being cut – just be sure that both cuts meet in the middle!

Fig. 91 Using guide rails with a portable circular saw. (Atlas Copco Tools Limited)

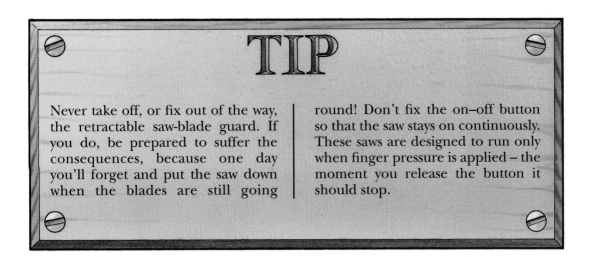

TIP

Never take off, or fix out of the way, the retractable saw-blade guard. If you do, be prepared to suffer the consequences, because one day you'll forget and put the saw down when the blades are still going round! Don't fix the on–off button so that the saw stays on continuously. These saws are designed to run only when finger pressure is applied – the moment you release the button it should stop.

vertical position. If they have a fixed sole plate that won't allow angled cutting, then look for another. Reducing or increasing the depth of cut is usually achieved by pivoting the sole plate up or down at one end and then locking it off. This is particularly useful, especially when cutting through floorboards. Simple adjustable fences make ripping to width relatively easy. For those boards with waney, uneven edges, fix a straight-edge against which you can run the saw, or buy some dedicated guide rails (Fig. 91). An additional, occasional, optional extra is a table into which the saw can be inverted and fixed. This effectively turns it into a stand-alone circular saw bench.

Saw blades are normally supplied when buying new. However, when you come to replace them, be sure that you get the right bore size for your saw, because any movement on the spindle will render the whole thing potentially lethal. Blades are usually tungsten carbide tipped (TCT); this is a very hard and tough metal that will easily slice through a nail – although that course of action is not to be recommended!

The hand-held, portable circular saw is a useful addition to any workshop, and is a capable site worker as well. Moreover the various cordless saws now available, although of lesser capacity, are making them even more sought after. As with most things, you get what you pay for, but a middle capacity and priced saw will probably cover most needs.

PLANING, REBATING AND GROOVING

PLANING TOOLS

I have to admit that I don't use hand planes a great deal these days. For most commercial makers, time is a crucial factor, and I have found that my stand-alone over-and-under planes, saw benches and routers can quickly achieve most of what I want to do, without my having to lift a hand tool! This might alarm the purists, but I don't believe it will cause our traditional tools to become redundant. Invariably I still have to tidy up and finish off some parts of every job with hand tools, so it is still important that woodworkers should understand the basic principles associated with their use: then these can be applied in the most efficient

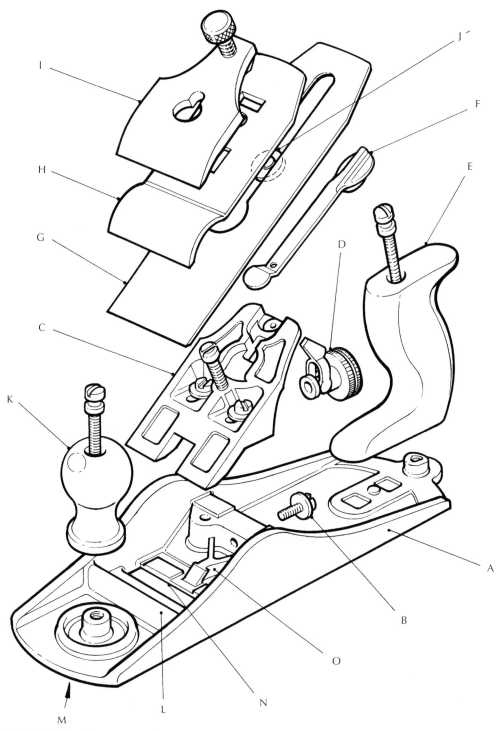

Fig. 92 All the bits that go to make up a hand plane: a: side body; b: frog-adjusting screw; c: frog; d: depth-adjusting nut; e: handle; f: lateral adjusting lever; g: cutter iron; h: cap iron; i: screw or lever cap; j: cap iron screw; k: front knob; l: web; m: sole; n: mouth; o: frog seating.

way possible, by hand or with powered assistance. To give hand planes the coverage they deserve would take another book, and there are others better equipped than I to do that.

Planes have been around for a long time: they come in all sorts of different shapes and sizes, and carry out a multitude of different functions, such as planing smooth, rebating, grooving and moulding. The most familiar of the older-style planes are made from wood, and if you go to any sale or auction you will invariably see examples on offer: maybe the simple, square-blocked smoothing or jack planes, more often the mass of special, purpose-made grooving and moulding planes. A lot of this kit was in continuous use right up to the 1950s and 1960s. More basic and simple in design, many still swear by them.

Modern, metal hand-planing tools will usually have some common component parts (Fig. 92). The plane illustrated is called a 'Bailey' plane after its designer, Leonard Bailey, who first patented it in 1858 – amongst the great many variations and different patterns available, this is still the most common. They are easier to adjust and set than their older counterparts (Fig. 93), having replaced

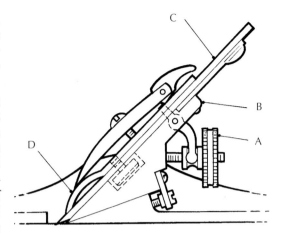

Fig. 93 Some plan details: a: the depth-adjusting nut lifts or lowers the blade and is attached to: b: the frog; c: the blade is moved by the adjuster fitting into the cap iron, d.

them, in the main, for general use. Shaping planes have been superseded by the router; however, with this latter tool the moulding shapes are restricted to those made by the manufacturer, whereas all those wooden moulding planes have an iron with a unique shape created by its maker – so if you don't want to be restricted, then buy these old ones when you can, and restore them.

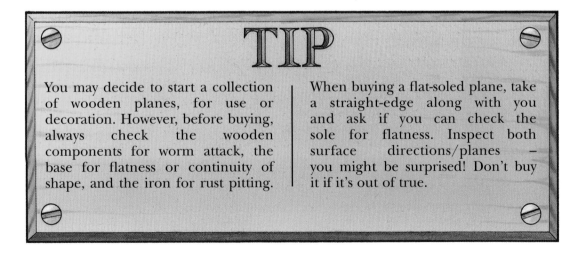

TIP

You may decide to start a collection of wooden planes, for use or decoration. However, before buying, always check the wooden components for worm attack, the base for flatness or continuity of shape, and the iron for rust pitting.

When buying a flat-soled plane, take a straight-edge along with you and ask if you can check the sole for flatness. Inspect both surface directions/planes – you might be surprised! Don't buy it if it's out of true.

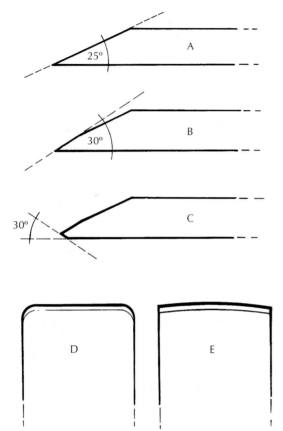

coarse or interlocked grain may sometimes be difficult. Back-grinding at 30 degrees (Fig. 94c) makes the iron more like a scraper, and is less likely to tear out the fibres of the grain. It also helps to maintain the cutting point when planing really hard woods because the angle is less acute – even with great care the corners of a straight cutting iron are likely to dig into a finished surface. There are two ways to grind the irons to avoid this and provide different surface finishes. To produce a finished surface, very slightly grind a radius on the corners of each iron (Fig. 94d): with this shape they will not dig in and ruin the surface. For coarse, heavy removal of shavings, a slight crown should be employed (Fig. 94e). Both these illustrations are exaggerated – the radii

Fig. 94 Some important cutter iron details: a: grinding angle; b: honing angle; c: back grinding for difficult materials; d: corner radiuses to avoid digging in; e: for coarse, thick cuts slightly curve the iron.

SETTING UP THE PLANE

Cutting irons, the blade, and their relationship to the cap iron are probably the most important factors affecting the quality of planing. For most general uses the iron should be ground at a constant 25 degrees (Fig. 94a); it should then be honed on an oilstone to a 30-degree cutting edge (Fig. 94b). If this is done lightly enough, the iron can be re-honed several times before there will be a need to re-grind. Getting a good finish on very

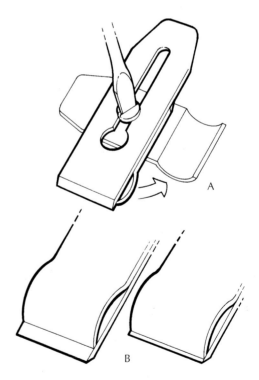

Fig. 95 The relationship between cap iron and cutter iron: a: loosen the screw and turn sideways to avoid damaging the edge; b: set back further for coarse cutting or closer for fine.

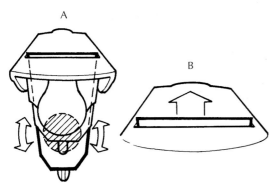

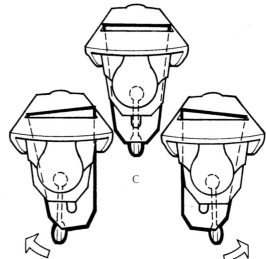

Fig. 96 Adjusting the cutting iron: a: invert the plane; b: wind the blade through until you can see it; c: sight down the sole and adjust the blade until it protrudes evenly by adjusting the lateral lever.

and crown should only be slight unless, as in the latter's case, you particularly want an uneven surface.

SETTING THE CAP IRON AND CUT

The cap iron is fitted to, or taken off the iron by releasing a bolt (Fig. 95). To avoid damaging the cutting edge when taking the cap iron off, always pull and turn it away to one side; reverse this action when replacing it. The distance the cap iron is set from the cutting edge will determine the thickness of shavings removed. With hardwoods it is best to reduce this to a minimum of around 0.5mm; for softwoods and bulk removal then set the cap iron at no more than 2mm (Fig. 95b). After positioning the assembled iron and cap iron onto the frog, locate the lever cap and tighten all into place. The cut setting through the mouth of the plane can now be made. Invert the plane and wind the adjuster screw until the blade starts to show below the sole. Eyeing down the sole, adjust the iron until it is parallel to the mouth using the lateral adjuster (Figs.

96a, b and c). Always finish this process by winding forwards and out, so that any slack is taken up on the thread. It is best to start planing with too little projection and then increase it as desired.

PLANING TECHNIQUE

The correct stance is important when planing. The workpiece should be at about waist height, allowing you to lean in during the cutting stroke. Position yourself above it, and start the stroke with the leading hand pressing down. As the stroke continues towards the end, move your body forwards from the waist as you go, and as each stroke is finished, transfer the hand pressure from front to back (Fig. 98a); by following this basic technique you will avoid rounding the ends of the planed surface. If it is a very long piece, do a bit at a time until nearly finished, then increase the length of stroke until you can walk the full length.

Planing wide pieces requires a slightly different technique. Plane the surface by 'slewing' the plane during the cutting

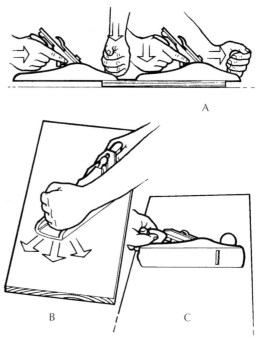

Fig. 98 Body position and action are important: a: start with pressure at the front, and switch as the cut follows through; b: for wider surfaces work progressively across it; and c: check it is flat with the edge of the plane.

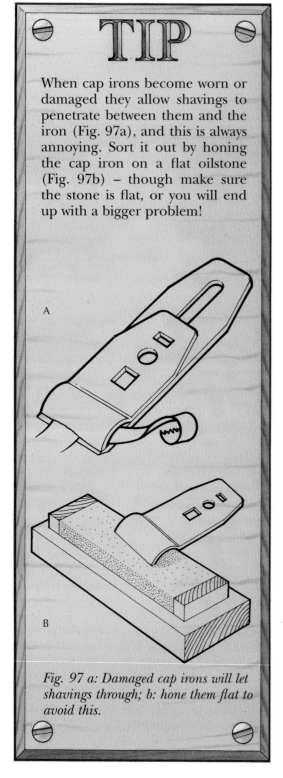

TIP

When cap irons become worn or damaged they allow shavings to penetrate between them and the iron (Fig. 97a), and this is always annoying. Sort it out by honing the cap iron on a flat oilstone (Fig. 97b) – though make sure the stone is flat, or you will end up with a bigger problem!

Fig. 97 a: Damaged cap irons will let shavings through; b: hone them flat to avoid this.

action (Fig 98b), and repeat this across the whole of the surface, checking regularly for flatness using the edge of the plane (Fig. 98c)

There are many different types and sizes of plane, and it is important to use the right one for the job – trying to achieve a straight surface with a short smoothing plane as opposed to a longer jack or jointing plane is not a good idea (Fig. 100). Planing end grain can also be a problem, and there are several solutions; the easiest is to plane into the centre from both sides (Fig. 101a). Always check for true with a try square until you've got it right. Another simple way is to clamp a piece of waste to the far edge of the surface being planed (Fig. 101b); be sure

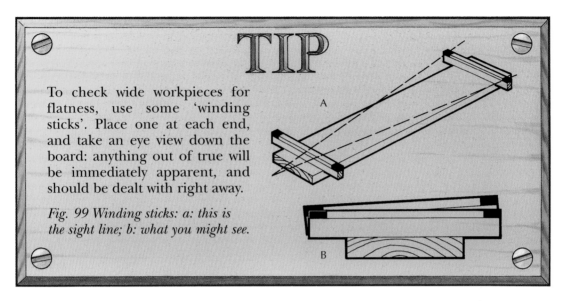

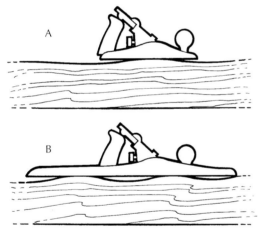

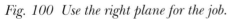

Fig. 100 Use the right plane for the job.

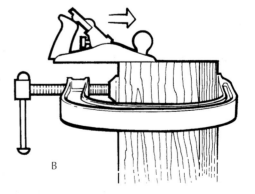

to have a stiff enough piece, clamped as close to the top as possible, to avoid even a small amount of break-out. The final alternative is to make a 'shooting' board, which should automatically give support to the back edge (Figs. 102a and b). Note that, even when using one of these techniques, it's always a good idea to cut a small bevel back to the line with a chisel just in case! The shooting-board concept can be adapted to produce some really

Fig. 101 Planing end grain can be difficult: a: work from the outside in; or, b: support the exit point with a stiff bit of waste.

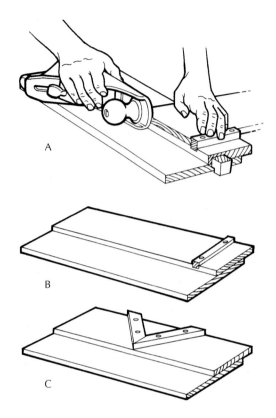

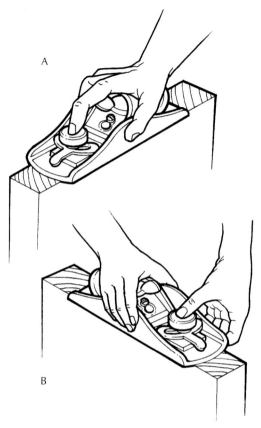

Fig. 102 a: End planing made easy with a shooting board; b: a simple shooting board;c: this shooting board can be used to clean up mitres.

Fig. 103 Use a block plane correctly: a: with one hand; or b: with two.

clean mitre joints (Fig. 102c). Smaller planes require a different holding position. The block plane, for example, is a one-handed job most of the time (Fig. 103a), though for even better support, try two (Fig. 103b).

TYPES OF PLANE

SMOOTHING PLANE

This is the shortest of the family of bench planes (Figs. 105c and d). Traditionally made about 5½–10in (140–255mm) long, the focus now seems to be concentrated on the longer end of this range. Cutter iron width can also vary, from about 1¾–2½in (45–65mm). As the name suggests, they are used for smoothing, or for the final finishing of a work. Particular care and attention should be paid to the sharpness and setting of the blade, to ensure that a good finish is achieved. And when you have completed the job, don't just plonk the plane sole plate down: try to tip it on its edge to avoid damage.

JACK PLANE

This is the 'Jack of all trades' plane for the initial planing down of rough-sawn materials (Fig. 105b). Jack planes used to range in length from about 10in

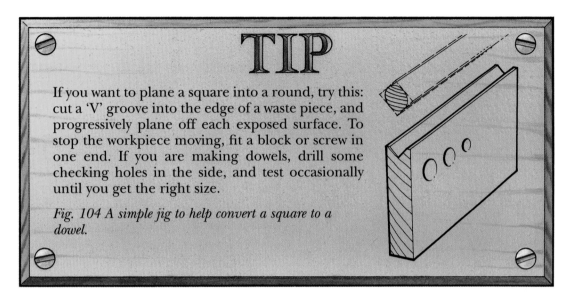

If you want to plane a square into a round, try this: cut a 'V' groove into the edge of a waste piece, and progressively plane off each exposed surface. To stop the workpiece moving, fit a block or screw in one end. If you are making dowels, drill some checking holes in the side, and test occasionally until you get the right size.

Fig. 104 A simple jig to help convert a square to a dowel.

(255mm) through to 15in (380mm), but like the smoothing plane, the focus now seems to be towards the longer lengths. The width of the cutter irons varies between 2in (50mm) to 2½in (65mm): the wider the plane, the more it will take off; therefore the narrower ones seem to be most popular. Some manufacturers groove the sole plate in order to reduce friction on rough and resinous surfaces.

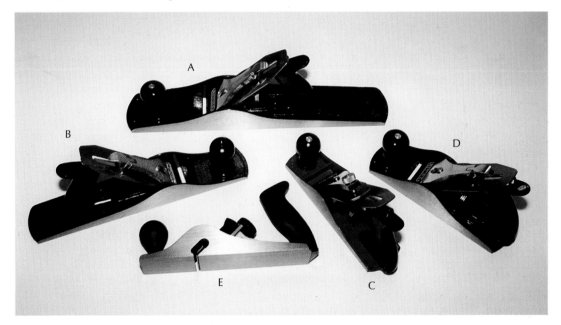

Fig. 105 A selection of hand planes: a: fore; b: jack; c: narrow smoothing; d: wide smoothing; e: replaceable blade.

Fig. 106 Block
planes: a: shoulder;
b: bull-nosed.

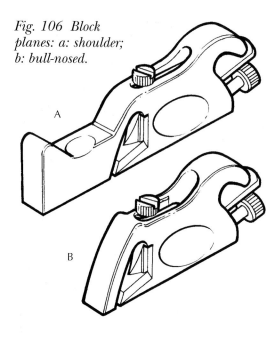

TIP

To help your plane run more easily across the working surface, rub a candle across its bottom; the candle wax will reduce friction between the plane and the wood.

Fig. 107 Block and model maker's planes: a: universal block plane; b: simpler version of the same; c: model maker's scraper, and d: block plane, and e: bull-nosed.

FORE PLANE

The fore plane is one of the big boys (Fig. 105a): traditionally their length spans the 18–20in (455–510mm) range, and cutter iron widths vary from 2–2½in (50–65mm). This is a mid-range plane that can occasionally be used instead of a jointer.

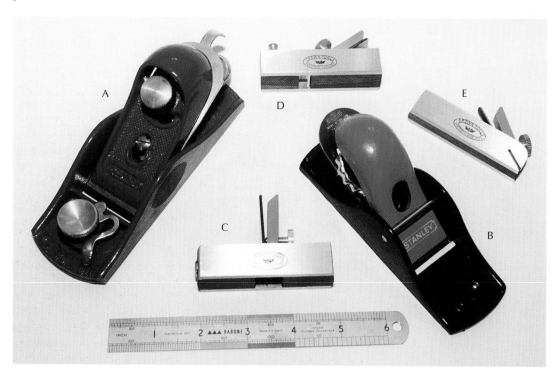

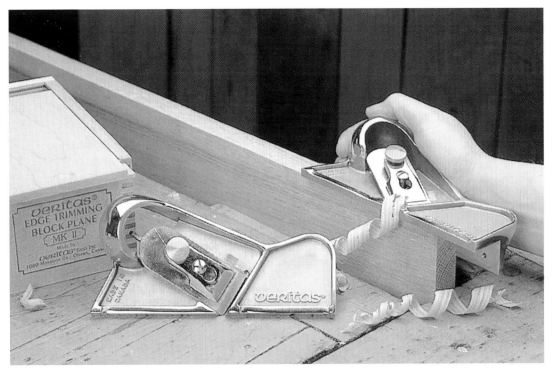

Fig. 108 An edge-trimming block plane. (BriMarc Associates)

JOINTER PLANE

The jointer plane has a very long sole plate, anything from 22in (560mm) up to 30in (760mm) long. The really long ones – 28in (710mm) to 30in (760mm) long – are called 'Try' planes in the UK. Today, jointer planes appear to be made in the shorter length range. Cutter iron widths vary from 2¼in (55mm) up to 2¾in (70mm). These planes are used to produce long, flat surfaces. The length of sole plate enables them to ride over any uneven surfaces, thus flattening them off. The longer planes are particularly useful when butt jointing, the extra length helping to ensure that there is a good straight joint – hence their name.

REPLACEABLE BLADE PLANE

You might like to consider one of these for larger rebating work (Fig. 105e): basically a smoothing plane with an open mouth, it can be used against a batten to create large rebates. The plane illustrated has a very useful replacement blade system, which saves you having to do any sharpening! It is supplied with spare blades with different profiles for various jobs.

BLOCK PLANES

These come in a great many sizes and shapes, although the following three designs are probably the most important. First, the shoulder plane (Fig. 106a), used to clean up shoulder joints such as tenons; some of these have a removable nose that turns them into bull-nosed planes. The bull-nosed plane (Fig. 106b) enables you to get quite close into

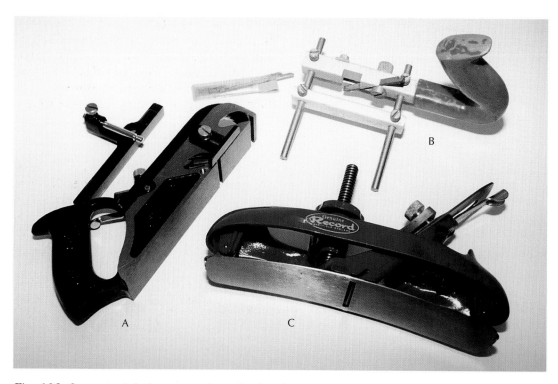

Fig. 109 Some special planes: a: rebate; b: plough; c: compass.

corners to clean up; it leaves only a small amount of chisel work because the iron is so close to the end. Third is the universal block plane (Fig. 107a and b), used for fine finishing, chamfering and similar jobs. They are all useful, though the latter will probably give you best value. There are a few block planes that have been designed for a specific purpose; for example, the edge-trimming plane (Fig. 108) has been designed to make sure the edge is a true 90 degrees to the face for jointing. A novel idea and, like a lot of small planes, it definitely has a place in the workshop.

MODEL MAKER'S PLANES

For interest, I thought it would be fun to include these small planes (Fig. 107c, d and e) – for the model maker, however, these are serious bits of kit. The three shown are a smoothing plane, a bull-nosed plane and a scraper plane respectively, and as you can see, they are not very large, only 3in (75mm) long. They are sat on my bookcase as I write, and I can assure you, they do work!

REBATE PLANES

Sometimes called 'rabbet' planes, from the Old French rabattre meaning 'to reduce', thus 'cut out a rebate'. They are designed to cut rebates up to the width of their bodies, normally about 1½in (40mm) (Fig. 109a). They usually have width and depth stops to allow precision cutting, and a 'spur' attachment that helps to ensure the side cut is clean. A useful feature with this one is that the cutter iron can be mounted some way forward, thus turning it into a bull-nosed plane.

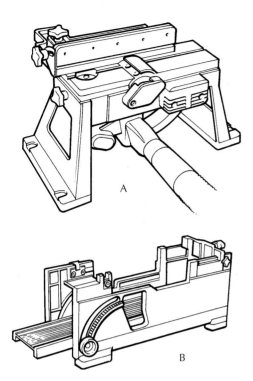

A

B

Fig. 110 a: This is a typical purpose-made stand into which a powered plane can be inverted. b: This purpose-made stand allows the portable plane to become a thicknesser.

PLOUGH PLANES

These are designed to plough grooves of various widths (Fig. 109b). The one illustrated is made up with a light alloy body and came with a selection of cutters; more expensive versions are available, with up to ten different cutters. Using the guides supplied, grooves can be cut 5in (125mm) or so from the edge; in most cases the depth will be limited to about ¾in (19mm).

COMBINATION PLANES

The combination plane is of similar design to a plough plane, the only difference being that instead of straight cutters, the plane can be fitted with pre-shaped moulding cutters. These tools were the first real alternative to the old wooden moulding planes. For specialist moulding work they have their place, however they have been largely superseded by the router.

COMPASS PLANES

This is an extremely useful item of kit if you are going to be planing inner or outer curves (Fig. 109c). Devised by wheelwrights, it has a flexible steel sole plate that can be manipulated to fit convex and concave curves; the plate is adjusted to the required curve, and then the cut is set. Fitted with a standard cutter and cap iron, they are used as normal. They are quite expensive, therefore if you can find a secondhand one at the right price, buy it.

ELECTRIC PLANES

I have a couple of these, and when I want to 'ball' off a lot of shavings on something fixed in place or outside, I might reach for one (see earlier Fig. 90c and d). Otherwise my stand-alone planes carry out most of the things that I need to do. Most of the power planes can be put in the same class as a jack plane: use them to remove the sawn surfaces of timber, but finish off with something else. Some do have attachments for rebating, others can be inverted in a stand to use as a surface planer (Fig. 110a). Another optional accessory on some of the heavier duty models turns the whole thing into a thicknesser (Fig. 110b).

There are certain features to look for when buying an electric plane. First, the width of cut can vary; it's probably a good idea not to buy one that is too narrow. Motor size is not desperately important unless you are aiming to use the plane a lot – something in the region of 400 to 500

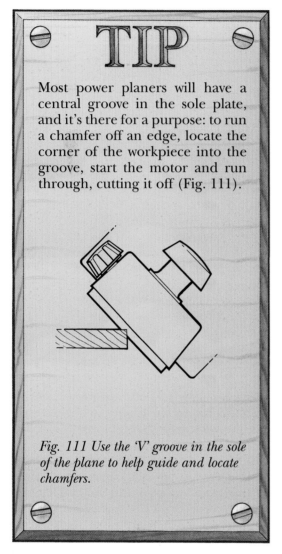

TIP

Most power planers will have a central groove in the sole plate, and it's there for a purpose: to run a chamfer off an edge, locate the corner of the workpiece into the groove, start the motor and run through, cutting it off (Fig. 111).

Fig. 111 Use the 'V' groove in the sole of the plane to help guide and locate chamfers.

watts should be sufficient to tackle most jobs. The lighter machines usually have a maximum depth of cut of about 2mm (¹⁄₁₆in), which is not very taxing; industrial versions, with 4–5mm (⅛–³⁄₁₆in) cuts,

should have motors that are proportionally larger. Look carefully at the sole plate construction: if you want to do some rebating, check that the model you are interested in is capable of doing this. Side fences are not always supplied, so check if they are an optional extra. Blades should be double-edged to extend their life; they can be in HSS or TCT. Some fancy blade options are available that produce a rustic finish! Look at the exit port for the waste: even with an extractor fitted, one of mine blocks up if I get carried away. Finally, if you want to turn it into a surfacer and or thicknesser, then check that the one you are considering can have these fittings as options; it's too late when you get it home.

PLANING TECHNIQUE

The freehand use and control of a powered planer is similar to standard practice. Hold the front end firmly on the workpiece to start, engage the motor, and move forwards. As the end of the cut approaches, switch emphasis to the trailing hand to ensure that you don't get a 'dig-in' – however, I can tell you that this often happens! Take care not to let your fingers wander underneath. Most of the cutter blocks, although small, are whizzing around at a considerable speed, producing anything from twenty to thirty thousand cuts per minute (CPM). Treated with respect, however, these planes – and in particular the lightweight ones – can be a useful and willing workhorse around the place for many years.

— 5 —

SHAPING, SCRAPING AND SANDING

The tools described here are hammer-graded as in previous chapters, on the same scale from one to five, indicating the least to the most essential, and the most practical to buy initially on a limited budget.

SPOKESHAVES

The classification 'shaves' covers a multitude of different types of hand tool. It includes the draw knife, already discussed; scrapers and routers, described later; and those we will concentrate on here, the spokeshave. Spokeshaves were not necessarily designed for shaping spokes, as their name might suggest; in fact they were used by a variety of trades including coopers, coachbuilders, chair makers, wainwrights and, of course, wheelwrights. Each of these groups would have produced their own specific tool for different jobs – and that is one of the main reasons why you will always find a number of wooden spokeshaves at local auctions and sales.

The spokeshave has features similar to a bench plane, namely a sole and a cutter iron, or blade, held in place by a cap iron. There are two differences, however: first is the way it is held, in that the hands must be side by side; and second, the short sole makes it a great deal more flexible when shaping corners and rounds. The older wooden spokeshaves tend to wear out rather quickly, thus requiring greater maintenance, therefore metal-bodied ones were introduced and have become popular. In both cases, to adjust the depth of cut, tap the blade until the desired projection is reached. The newer, generally straight-blade versions have a pair of knurled screw adjusters, which makes things a lot easier. Spokeshaves are very helpful to have around the workshop, especially when you want to run a quick chamfer onto something; nor are they desperately expensive, so don't dismiss them out of hand!

Look out for the following when you are thinking of buying: in the older wooden types, beware of worm attack – if you see any exit holes, then I should avoid that particular tool. Check the mouth, where the blade protrudes through the sole; wooden spokeshaves have a tendency to wear in this region a lot. Apply a straight-edge – a short steel rule is quite acceptable – across the width of the mouth, and see if the latter is hollowed; if the wear is too great, you will need to restore it. The better metal spokeshaves have a malleable iron body – meaning they are made of cast iron that has been heated and cooled under controlled conditions to render the metal less brittle. The weak point is where the handles join the body. Some new spokeshaves will have a lifetime guarantee, and these are probably the best to buy. Also, if you have a choice between manual or screw adjustment of the blade, choose the latter.

Finally, be careful to buy the right spokeshave for the job: for this, refer to the descriptions below.

TYPES OF SPOKESHAVE

STANDARD, FLAT SOLE SPOKESHAVE

As its name suggests, this has a flat sole and a straight blade (Fig. 112b), and is ideal for simple rounding work or for creating chamfers. Some models have side fences that allow a constant 45-degree angle to be planed: the fence rides on the adjacent flat surface and guides the spokeshave from this. They are also capable of planing round the outside of a convex shape; however, unfortunately they won't do an internal concave shape.

Fig. 112 Some spokeshaves: a: curved sole; b: straight adjustable.

Fig. 113 A half-round spokeshave. (BriMark Associates)

ROUND SOLE SPOKESHAVE

For internal curves, one of these is a must (Fig. 112a). As with the standard model, it incorporates a straight blade and can have screw adjusters; the difference is the convex sole plate that allows the internal cuts to be made. A compass plane is an alternative, but this spokeshave will get into tighter radii.

HALF-ROUND SPOKESHAVE

As the name suggests, these tools have a special concave body, side to side, with a blade to match (Fig. 113). They are ideal for creating rounds on, say, chair components, and come with a variety of radii. Obviously they are not as easy to maintain as the straight-bladed spokeshave, so this needs to be taken into consideration if buying. Don't forget that the standard tool can also cut a round; however, it does have the disadvantage of leaving a small, flat surface that may need to be sanded off.

RADII SPOKESHAVE

The opposite of a half-round spokeshave: the sole and blade are made with a convex shape that allows hollows to be planed. In fact I have yet to be challenged with a job that needs a tool like this, but you never know!

COMBINATION SPOKESHAVE

This tool usually combines a slightly smaller, standard, straight spokeshave with a half-round one, both in the same body, the idea behind it being to provide greater flexibility. For instance, you might be working on a project that requires both flat and curved cuts simultaneously, and with one of these you will not have to keep changing over.

FILES, RASPS AND SURFORMS

Not every woodworking workshop will need a complete range of these tools, but a couple will always be useful – files, for instance, will always be needed, especially if you use scrapers, although they are not very efficient at actually removing wood. Shaped files can be used to improve the finish on a surface after rasping. Rasps are really quite vicious, as the face that attacks the wood is made up of teeth that dig in, removing a small shaving or chip as you work them. As a result, the quality of the finished surface is very poor; however, they are ideal for the fast removal of waste on shaped work. Carvers are probably those most likely to use rasps. I used to make replacement gun stocks, and found them invaluable for balling off the main of the waste, especially round the pistol grip and cheek plates.

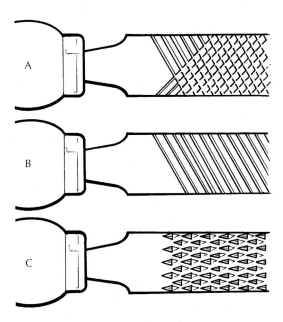

Fig. 114 Different types of cut on files: a: double; b: single; c: rasp.

Solid metal-bodied files and rasps are classified by 'cut', files with double and single cuts (Fig 114a and b), and rasps as 'rasp cut' (Fig. 114c). Both files and rasps are further classified by the depth, or coarseness, of these cuts into the body, files as smooth, medium, coarse and bastard; and rasps as smooth, second-cut and bastard. Naturally in both cases the last one is pretty rough! Solid-bodied rasps have been developed into plane-like tools with thin blades, universally called 'surforms'. The blade is housed in a frame with a thin metal rasp plate for its sole. This sole is in reality a detachable blade that has been punctured with regular-sized teeth. These face forwards into the direction of cut the tool is used in. The advantage of the surform over the traditional rasp is the fact that it doesn't clog up so much: the shavings or chips pass through the tooth holes and can usually be extracted easily. Even so, some of the smaller ones still clog up, and you need to keep your eye on them at all times.

FILES

To have a few of these in the workshop is always useful. I have a boxful gathered over the years that don't see the light of day often – but when I want one I know where they are. For those starting out I would suggest choosing a couple of each in half-round and square bodies, probably with a full range of coarseness. Some variation between small and large would also be useful.

SOLID-BODIED RASP

Rasps are not likely to be used very much, so maybe only a couple need be added to the toolbox. Some smallish, half-round ones again, possibly with a smooth and a bastard cut.

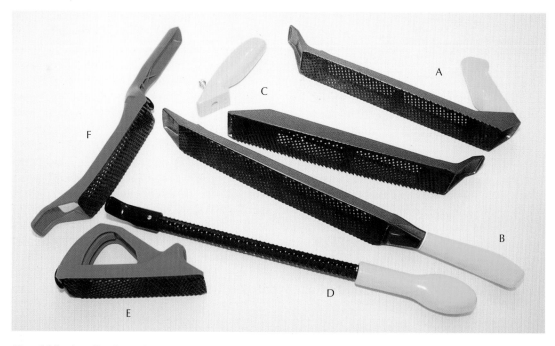

Fig. 115 A collection of rasps and surforms: a: plane-type surform; b: file style; c: detachable handle; d: round; e: small economy; f: file economy.

SURFORMS

Out of choice I would always go for a surform, rather than a solid rasp, when contemplating larger work. Most manufacturers make these tools as versatile as possible. They may look like a plane, but usually the handle is detachable and reversible so they can then be used as a file (Fig. 115a and c). Individual tools are also available; some will look like flat and round files (Fig. 115b and d). This first group is well built and fairly substantial, though economy versions are available with plastic bodies (Fig. 115e and f); for occasional use this latter group will probably be more than sufficient for most purposes. When buying a surform, check that the model you want has replaceable blades, and that you can get them with different types of cut. One maker has at least six different types of cut blades for various jobs.

POWERED RASPS

Rasps specifically made for power tools come in all sorts of different shapes and sizes. Most will be purpose made to fit into either a drill or a jigsaw – though how much good they do the bearings on these tools, I'm not quite sure! One of the most common is a straight bit for a drill (Fig. 116a): this can be used to penetrate, and then enlarge a hole, or to create a slot. The round one is for hollowing (Fig. 116b), and could probably also be used as a countersink.

ROUTERS

Of all the tools described in this book, the router must be one of the most versatile to be carried forward from the twentieth century. In recent years we have all enjoyed the benefits brought by the

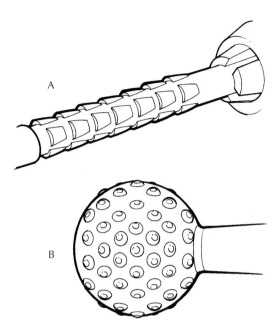

Fig. 116 A couple of odd powered rasps: a: drill bit type; b: ball.

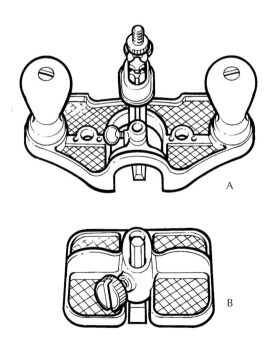

Fig. 117 Hand-held and driven routers: a: fully adjustable; b: a simple thumb one.

increased availability and versatility of the powered router, and our appreciation of this magnificent tool can only grow. When you think about it, it is truly remarkable how much just one piece of equipment, fitted with the right cutter and accessory, can achieve, and in the few short pages of this book I will never be able to do full justice to its capabilities, or cover comprehensively all its features. However, to understand its present form we must first take a brief look at how it developed.

The precursor to our modern, powered router was called the 'old woman's tooth', mentioned in Chapter 1 (and see also Fig. 2), and this is how it all started: a moulded block of wood with a protruding cutter iron. The name is derived from the action of pigs that 'root' things out – thus 'rout out'. If you come across one of these older style, wooden routers in a sale it may be worth your while acquiring it; I have never seen one and I believe they are quite rare. Their function was to dig out the waste in a trench across the grain; because of their design it is relatively easy to set the depth required, and for stopped trenches they were ideal as they could clean the waste right out to the end. Metal-framed routing planes are still made, and are still available today (Fig. 117a and b): the simpler design is gripped and propelled by fingers and thumbs; the other has two on-board wooden knobs. This latter router plane is slightly larger and more refined, with better cutter blade adjustment.

Let us move on to the modern and extremely desirable powered routers. My first router was an old 'Stanley' (Fig.118a) with an 1120-watt motor and a single speed of 27,000rpm; it takes cutters with ¼in (6mm) shaft, and is a fixed body type which requires the depth of cut to be adjusted by a screw ring. When entering a central cut the body must be tilted and then lowered to engage the cutter. Later I bought a second-hand Elu MOF96 plunge

Fig. 118 Powered routers come in all shapes and sizes: a: my old 'Stanley'; b: medium- to heavy-duty 12mm chuck 'Skil'; c: one of DeWalts with a 12mm chuck; d: light- to medium-weight 'AEG'; e: one of the lightweight 'Z' range from 'Hitachi'.

router. The plunge action allows the cutter depth to be set, and the router is then positioned over the workpiece and plunged into it to start the cutting action; a great improvement over the other one. The Elu could also be inverted in its own stand, effectively becoming a spindle moulder. This second router also has a single speed, of 24,000rpm, a 600-watt motor and a ¼in (6mm) cutter shaft.

By this time I was beginning to realize how versatile these machines are. A few years later I invested in a Bosch 1300 ACE plunge router, a marvellous tool with all

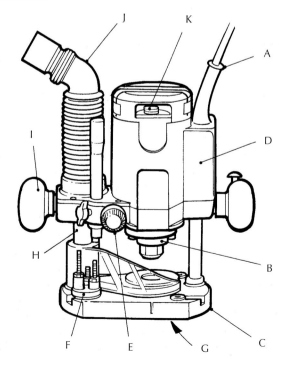

Fig. 119 (right) Some routers will have common features: a: power cable; b: chuck; c: base plate; d: part metal or plastic body; e: depth stop fine adjuster; f: depth stop carousel; g: base plate face; h: pillars; i: locking handle; j: chipping exhaust; k: adjustable speed control.

the modern features, including variable speed, 12–24,000rpm with soft start, 1300-watt motor, interchangeable collets of 6mm, 8mm and 12mm, and fine vertical and lateral adjustments. More recently another state-of-the-art router has been acquired, this one with a 1400-watt motor (Fig. 118b). I use the old Stanley for those simple outer-edge jobs, the Elu is permanently inverted in its stand ready for use, and the two newer routers have to cope with everything else. I also have innumerable home-made jigs, put together to satisfy particular jobs; my pride and joy is a 'Leigh' D4 dovetail jig.

There are routers to suit everyone's needs and pocket. Of the huge variety available – indeed, every manufacturer will probably have a whole selection – only a few are illustrated here (Fig. 118c, d and e). Apart from the fixed overhead or inverted routers, most hand-held tools will have, in the main, common features (Fig. 119); the more important of those associated with the portable ones are discussed below. As always, you should look for and select the machine that matches your needs, and buy the best you can afford.

MOTOR SIZE, SPEEDS, SWITCHES AND CABLES

Motor sizes may be broadly classified into three categories, namely light, medium, and heavy or industrial use. These must not be taken in isolation, however, as collet size and the type of work to be carried out will also influence the size of motor required. But generally speaking, motors of up to 600–700 watts will drop into the first group, 800–1200 or 1300 into the middle one, and anything over can be classed at an industrial rating. So when considering what size motor to buy, think through the amount of work you are likely to carry out with your router.

Motor speed – known as rpm, or revolutions per minute – will, ideally, be variable, and the reason for this is simple. Consider, for instance, a small diameter cutter: its 'peripheral' speed, the rpm at which the outer part travels, will not be much different to that of the inner part, whereas a large cutter has a much faster peripheral speed. With the latter, the motor can go more slowly to compensate – in fact if it travels too fast, all that will happen is that the wood will burn! A comfortable range of rpm to cope with most jobs and cutters will be between 10–25,000 rpm. Any speeds higher than this will also be acceptable.

Most modern routers will have a swivel or dial speed control, which you set at the desired level before starting. Incorporated within the handles/knobs will probably be the on–off switch. Ideally this will have a 'soft start' facility, meaning that as you engage the motor it will start slowly, then increase the rpm steadily until it reaches the pre-set speed. This is a good feature, though make sure the motor has reached its full, designated operating speed before you engage the cutter in the workpiece. Some of the older, larger machines used to try and tear your hands off until they got going! Check the cable length and size, too: a thin, poor-looking cable will probably break down and fracture quickly. Aim for a cable length of 10–12ft (3–4m); anything shorter is bound to require an extension at some point.

COLLETS AND LOCKING MECHANISMS

The collet is directly related to the shaft size of the cutter, and is usually 6mm, 8mm or 12mm (Fig. 120). Most will have a self-locking mechanism that works as you tighten the collet nut. Logically routers that will accept 12mm collets can take smaller ones, but not vice versa! The majority of cutters have 6mm shafts, but

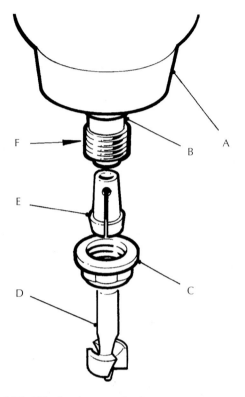

Fig. 120 The business end of a router: a: body; b: chuck; c: collet nut; d: cutter; e: collet; f: thread on the motor-driven spindle to take collet nut.

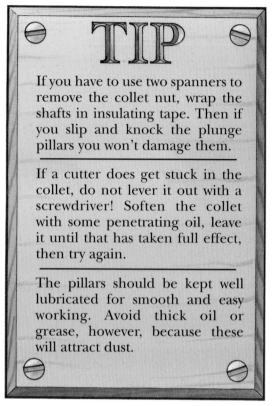

TIP

If you have to use two spanners to remove the collet nut, wrap the shafts in insulating tape. Then if you slip and knock the plunge pillars you won't damage them.

If a cutter does get stuck in the collet, do not lever it out with a screwdriver! Soften the collet with some penetrating oil, leave it until that has taken full effect, then try again.

The pillars should be kept well lubricated for smooth and easy working. Avoid thick oil or grease, however, because these will attract dust.

the specialist and larger ones will be manufactured with 8mm or 12mm shafts. If you wish to obtain total flexibility, then it is essential you have a router that will accept a larger collet – though check with the manufacturer that it will also take the smaller ones. The advantage of the larger collet is that it can take a more robust cutter; and the larger the shaft size, the better grip the collet can make on it. Small shafts can flex and distort occasionally. Whatever size of cutter is fitted, the shaft should always be inserted along at least three-quarters of its length before the collet is tightened; and always check that the cutter is not grounded (not touching any part of the body).

Collets tend to get neglected and abused; however it is important to take particular care of them. Always keep them clean and lightly oiled; if they are clogged up with dirt and grease they will not function correctly. Most of this can be softened in a light oil or diesel, and then wire-brushed off. If they get rusted, the collets will become pitted and you should consider replacing them. Long runs will eventually create metal fatigue leading to failure, so it is always better to buy a new collet rather than risk having a cutter fly out! Never leave your collet tightened into place without a cutter, as it may distort. Also, don't leave a cutter set up in the collet for too long, unless you know it's well oiled, as you may have difficulty getting it out.

The locking mechanisms on some routers are surprisingly complicated. My old Stanley has a motor spindle lock at the top and one spanner that works on the collet nut; the Elu has to use two spanners! Why can't the process be kept simple? Check this carefully on a potential purchase, and if it is complicated then look elsewhere.

TO PLUNGE OR NOT TO PLUNGE?

In reality this is not an option, as only older, second-hand machines will not have a plunge action. If, however, you are offered an old router, then don't refuse it, because all you need do is perfect a slightly different technique in order to realize its full potential. The important thing is to check that the plunge pillars, or legs, are well engineered and fit into their housings correctly, so look out for wobble and play. The pillars should be polished or chromed, and the return spring should still have the strength to pull the router out of the workpiece when released. Check all these factors.

DEPTH GAUGES AND SIDE FENCES

Depth gauges are more sophisticated that they used to be. Most will have a carousel or turret system of multi-level stops on the topside of the base plate, and a sliding bolt or bar can be locked against these with, in most cases, some sort of fine screw adjustment. Check what is on offer: can you see how easy it is to use? Will it provide the sort of fine adjustment you might need? Is it robust enough not to slip? Look to see how the depth, or plunge, setting can be locked into place; this will be via a lever, knob or one of the handles. Does it lock tight, and is it substantial enough to stop any slippage? This is a crucial part of your prospective router, so pay attention to it.

Side fences follow a similar pattern. Most are fitted to the router on a pair of round bars; these are locked to the base plate, and the adjustment is made on the outboard side. The better routers will have a fine wheel adjustment facility, and it is important to check that this works

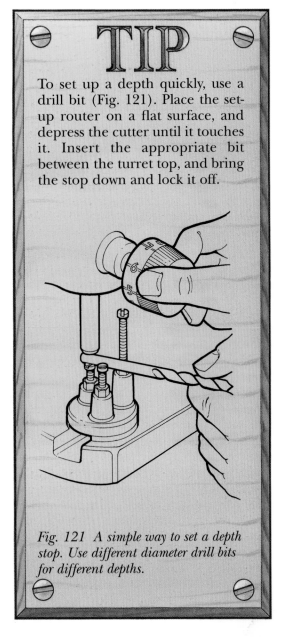

TIP

To set up a depth quickly, use a drill bit (Fig. 121). Place the set-up router on a flat surface, and depress the cutter until it touches it. Insert the appropriate bit between the turret top, and bring the stop down and lock it off.

Fig. 121 A simple way to set a depth stop. Use different diameter drill bits for different depths.

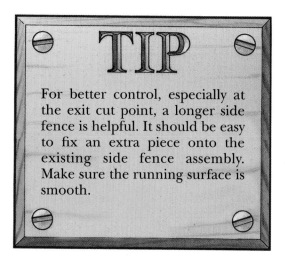

For better control, especially at the exit cut point, a longer side fence is helpful. It should be easy to fix an extra piece onto the existing side fence assembly. Make sure the running surface is smooth.

satisfactorily. The surface of the fence that runs adjacent to the workpiece should also be inspected, to be sure that it is smooth enough to generate minimum friction. Thin, weak bars and a poor fence construction can cause a great deal of grief.

BASE PLATES AND GUIDE BUSHES

The base plate is an important part of the router: for precision, it needs to be securely fitted with a smooth surface at right angles to the motor drive/cutter shaft. It may be totally round, like my old Stanley, or – more commonly – elliptical in shape with two parallel straight sides. The outer circumference of the base plate has to be exactly centred, end to end and side to side, to avoid any slight discrepancies in moulding size during use. A lot of router work will require the base plate to be run up a batten or guide, so it is an important part of the construction. The centre hole needs to be big enough to allow the collet to pass through; if it is not, then it should have a removable section to let this happen. Some jigs will require extra projection beyond the base plate, so this centre hole

clearance is important. Check the type and number of fittings, too: is the plate securely attached? Can it be inverted easily and fixed to a table? The simpler it is, the better.

Guide bushes of various types, sizes and shapes are available (Fig. 122). They are fitted to the base plate and used in conjunction with a 'follower' in various jigs and templates. Look to see how easy they are to fit, or indeed if they

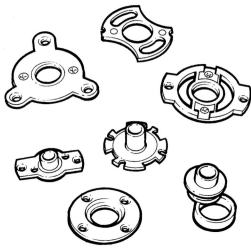

Fig. 122 Guide bushes are available to fit most routers.

There may be instances when a larger or different shaped base plate will be useful. If you make them up yourself, then try and use a clear plastic of at least 6mm or thicker. The see-through base will give you increased visibility.

can be fitted; though older routers can be modified to take bushes. Find a friendly local engineer who can adapt the base plate for you if you are intending to use jigs.

VISIBILITY, FEEL AND EXTRACTION

Modern routers are invariably supplied with a plastic shield to protect the operator from dust and dirt. However, I find that I still get covered, and because I wear glasses, it is sometimes difficult to see even when hooked up to the extraction system. I think it's important to see what's going on. If you remove the shield, make sure you wear safety glasses and a face mask. I have overcome the problem of visibility by wearing a full-face respirator hood that filters the air; it's a great bit of kit, but hot in summer! But then if I check round the business end of the router to make sure there is no clutter I can at least see something of what is going on.

The router needs to feel comfortable. If you are going to move it frequently, then it will not want to be too heavy; on the other hand, a light machine might judder whilst in use. Tidy up trailing cables by hanging them over your shoulder or suspending them from something relatively high whilst the router is in use; whatever system you think of, try it out to see if it is effective.

Extraction is important, the act of diverting as much waste and dust away from you as well as the router (the health and safety implications are discussed later). A good-sized extraction port is essential, as one that is too small will easily clog. Think through how the extraction tube will be fitted to the port: will it get in the way whilst routing and impede the cut? How is the waste going to get out? Is it via that shield you have just taken off to improve visibility? If it is, put it back on again.

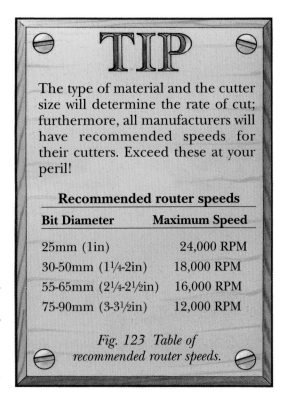

TIP

The type of material and the cutter size will determine the rate of cut; furthermore, all manufacturers will have recommended speeds for their cutters. Exceed these at your peril!

Recommended router speeds

Bit Diameter	Maximum Speed
25mm (1in)	24,000 RPM
30-50mm (1¼-2in)	18,000 RPM
55-65mm (2¼-2½in)	16,000 RPM
75-90mm (3-3½in)	12,000 RPM

Fig. 123 Table of recommended router speeds.

CUTTERS AND TECHNIQUES

The range and variety of cutters is so huge that it is difficult to know where to start. However, you will obviously buy cutters to fit your router: with a 6mm collet their range is significant; with an 8mm or 12mm it is considerably more. Whether you choose smaller or larger collets will depend on the work to be carried out, and how versatile you want the router to be. Just be aware that a lot of waste removal, the consequence of long and/or deep patterns, requires a more gutsy motor and cutter, whereas light, occasional work can be covered by the smaller sizes. Remember, too, that larger mouldings can be built up from a series of smaller cutters.

There are several different types of cutter, all designed to carry out a specific function or produce a unique moulding; a few of the common ones are illustrated here (Figs. 124 and 125). The vast

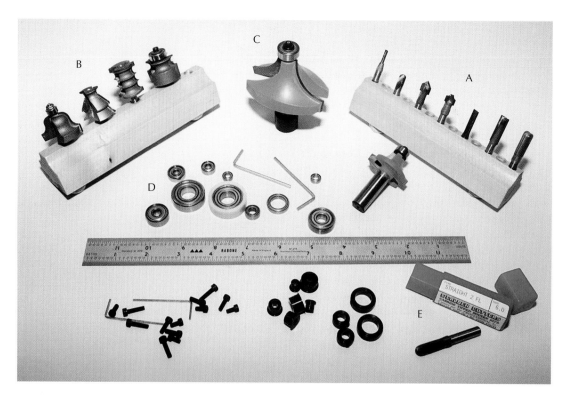

Fig. 124 (above). Router cutters and guides: a: simple straight or small profiles; b: fancy profiles; c: large round over; d: a range of guide roller bearings; e: most cutters will come packed in wax.

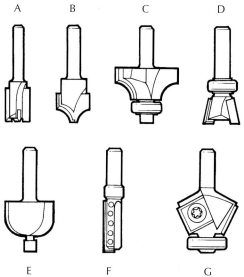

Fig. 125 Different types of router cutter: a: straight; b: profile; c: top roller bearing; d: bottom roller bearing; e: integral guide pin; f: straight replaceable cutters; g: angled, roller-bearing replaceable cutters.

majority will have an edge tipped with hardened steel, HSS or TCT, and some professional cutters may be made from solid HSS or TCT; others will have some form of diamond tipping. Obviously this latter group will be more expensive. An interesting development has been the replaceable tip cutter, whereby thin, straight or pre-shaped cutters can be disposed of, once worn, and replaced (Fig. 125f and g). Those cutters likely to keep their edge longer will usually cost more. None are cheap, however, so look after them. Cutters are generally supplied covered in wax (Fig. 124e), to protect the edges from damage. You should also try to prevent them from making contact with

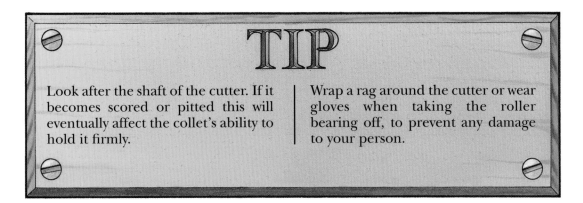

each other, by keeping them in a rack or box: the cutting edges are brittle and will chip easily.

Simple straight or profile cutters (Figs. 124a, 125a and b) are designed for use with a fence; roller bearing cutters (Figs. 124c, 125c and d) are designed for freehand operation and will follow an edge. A wide range of different sized bearings are available (Fig. 124d). By changing the bearing you may increase or decrease the depth of profile produced by the cutter. Some other edge-forming cutters will have a guide pin incorporated into the end that is used to follow a former or jig (Fig. 125e); these are generally used with fixed head routers.

This description of cutters cannot possibly do them full justice. The best way forward is probably to collect a range of cutter manufacturers' brochures and price lists; you can then select the right cutter for the job at the most competitive price.

ROUTING TECHNIQUES

It is important to follow a few simple techniques and rules when using a portable router. When viewed from above, with the body of the router between you and the cutter, the cut direction is clockwise. To get the best from the cutting action, in most circumstances the router

needs to be moved around in the opposite direction for external cuts (Figs. 126a and 127a); the opposite rule should be applied with internal cuts (Fig. 126b). This means you will have to make a positive effort to initiate the cutting sequence, because if you stop pushing, the router will go nowhere. If, however, the router is fed in the direction of cut the situation changes dramatically, because the cutter will then dig in and take charge, and attempt to remove too much waste too quickly.

When you are cutting grooves, trenches or moulds along or across the grain, the action is balanced in most cases. Plunge down in a sweeping action, moving into the direction of cut, making sure you are at the desired depth before entering the workpiece. If executing a stopped trench,

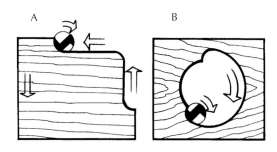

Fig. 126 The direction of cut is important: a: start at 1 on the outside and work round anti-clockwise; b: internally start on the end grain and work in a clockwise direction.

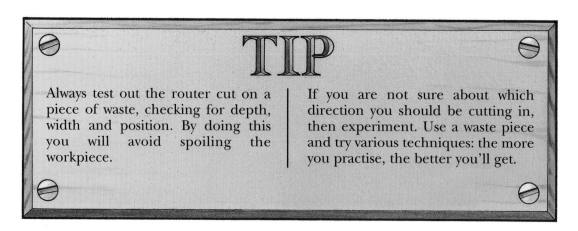

TIP

Always test out the router cut on a piece of waste, checking for depth, width and position. By doing this you will avoid spoiling the workpiece.

If you are not sure about which direction you should be cutting in, then experiment. Use a waste piece and try various techniques: the more you practise, the better you'll get.

then plunge down and enter, sweeping forwards again; carry the cut through, then return to the starting point, in the reverse direction, to clean up. In all these cases there are two further rules. First, never try to take too much off in one go: little and often is the order of the day. Second, lead into the cut and keep moving: if you stop, the cutter will whizz round and burn the profile. If you have to exit, then go back or away from the leading edge.

In the same way, fixed overhead or inverted routers have a code of procedure to protect the safety of the operator (Fig. 127a and b). Once again the cutting action will grab the workpiece if it is fed in the wrong direction, and it is sometimes best to observe the following technique: when moulding around a workpiece, start by cutting the end grain first. Inevitably there will be some 'break-out' as the router exits the cut because the cutter will tend to split out the last few bits of grain, but by starting across the grain, all this break-out can be tidied away with the next cut. Therefore work logically: end grain, straight grain, end grain and a final clean-up on the straight grain. The same applies to all types of routing, fixed or portable.

Having said all this, there are, nevertheless, occasions when you can legitimately go in the 'wrong' direction! I call this 'climb' cutting, and there are

various reasons why you might choose this angle of attack – primarily because otherwise perhaps you can't get at, or into, a specific position. One thing is for sure – you will know when you are doing it, and must be prepared: hanging on to the router when it tries to run away is a good start! In most cases climb cutting will only, sensibly, be taking off a small amount of waste; for instance, sometimes a finishing cut can produce a cleaner surface when you run the wrong way back round a profile. The same technique will, occasionally, remove burn or ripple marks. There are two instances where it might be desirable to start with a climb cut. First, if you are only going to mould along one end-grain edge it will help to make a reverse cut on what would normally be the exit point. Climb cut a bit, then revert to the usual direction, and as the cut finishes it will enter the pre-cut section and not break out. Housing joints across the grain can be started in the same fashion. The alternative, in both cases, is to back up the exit cutting point with a substantial bit of waste.

IN SUMMARY

The router is therefore a truly remarkable tool: what else will cut and mould an internal hole or external panel, create

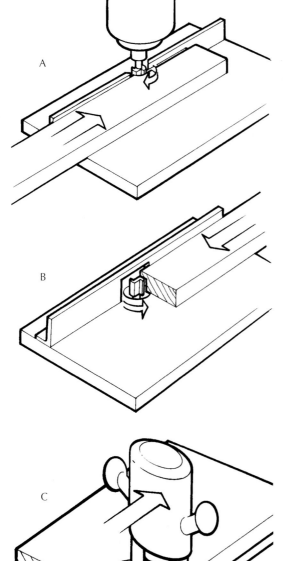

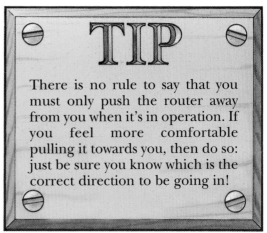

TIP

There is no rule to say that you must only push the router away from you when it's in operation. If you feel more comfortable pulling it towards you, then do so: just be sure you know which is the correct direction to be going in!

simple and complicated joints, plane, saw, and groove wood products? A spindle moulder probably comes closest, but it still can't do the internal bit without help! If you could have only one thing, a router would surely be the obvious choice. Certainly there are many other tools that will carry out some of the tasks better, more quickly and with more finesse, but I, for one, am very happy to have my routers even though I have some of these other machines!

Fig. 127 The router configuration determines the direction of feed: a: overhead; b: under-table; c: freehand.

TYPES OF ROUTER

HAND PORTABLE ROUTER

There is little more to say about these tools, bar reiterating that in my opinion the router is one of the most versatile bits of kit around. Take into account all the relevant factors discussed above, and go out and buy one.

FIXED OVERHEAD ROUTER

These are really industrial machines, though sometimes portable routers can be fitted to overhead slide arrangements to create a similar effect. Generally, with a much larger working table, big workpieces can be handled; also, repetitive production of components can be achieved efficiently and cost effectively. Simplistically a pattern is fitted to the workpiece, and this then follows a 'former' pin that projects above the table. The head of the router may be dropped into place, or the work run up to the cutter; in both cases the former pin is engaged by the pattern and the cut commenced. The job is done when the exit cut finishes at the end of the pattern. Always follow the usual rules of engagement for the direction of cut.

FIXED UNDER-TABLE ROUTER

For the general woodworker, a more useful facility is being able to invert a portable router. There are dedicated tables available made by individual manufacturers for one or more of their own routers, and there are specialist tables that will take a variety of routers made by different manufacturers. Basically the cutter projects above the table by a predetermined amount, and fences, guards and pressures adjusted accordingly. The workpiece is then fed through, and the mould, groove or rebate is cut. Alternatively, a workpiece can be moulded from all angles across a flat table using bearing-guided cutters; in this case the general rules about feed direction should be stringently observed.

SANDERS

There is a whole range of powered sanders on the market today, but let us start by looking at a couple of the traditional methods and some of the simpler systems.

Most of us at some stage will have completed the sanding process by using a bit of sandpaper wrapped around a wooden block, and this can be one of the most efficient ways of finishing off, especially in tight corners. A good way to maintain the original profile is to make a mirror image of the moulding and stick a bit of sandpaper to it. A step forwards would be to make or buy a felt-backed block (Fig. 128a), for comfort and longer paper life; this is because the give in the felt allows the paper to move slightly, thus avoiding excessive wear. Foam-filled sanding blocks, both flat and shaped, are also available (Fig. 128b); these can be used and then disposed of when fully clogged up or worn out. Some can have the paper replaced, others are flexible hand pads. The cost of all these should be considered, and compared with the simple wrapped paper versions.

The electric drill can form the basis for

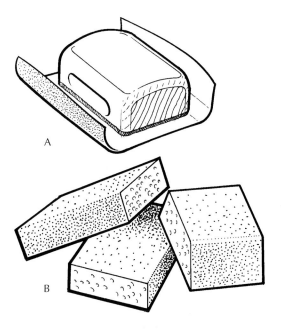

Fig. 128 Sanding blocks: a: home- or shop-made with thin felt face to help avoid tearing; b: softer, foam-filled, shop-bought, square or shaped.

a formidable sanding system. Orbital sanding attachments can be found to fit some makes and models, that simply clip over the business end of the drill and are used just like the purpose-made tool (Fig. 129a). However, you might like to consider the advantages of owning an orbital sander, because by the time you've bought the attachment and fiddled about fixing it up, it might actually be cheaper to get a dedicated sander that is always ready to use! Simple or slightly more sophisticated disc sanders can be fitted directly into the drill chuck (Fig. 129b). In addition to these there are some very

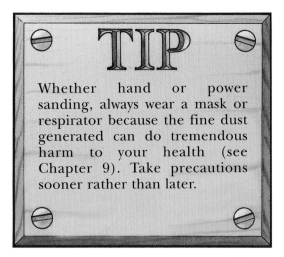

TIP

Whether hand or power sanding, always wear a mask or respirator because the fine dust generated can do tremendous harm to your health (see Chapter 9). Take precautions sooner rather than later.

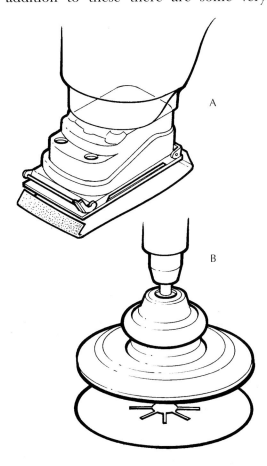

Fig. 129 Sanding attachments can be found: a: orbital sanding attachment for a drill; b: disc sander for a drill.

useful 'flap' sanders that can be chuck-mounted (Fig 130a and b); these are ideal for getting into awkward or restricted places. Take care when using these, however, because this type of sanding system tends to erode the original profile.

A number of drum sanding kits have come onto the market of late, and these are proving very successful. They are usually manufactured with a solid or an air-inflated drum, around which a sandpaper sleeve is fitted (Fig. 130c). These systems are very good for maintaining, as closely as possible, a truly round shape; they are also excellent for finishing off curves that have been cut on a bandsaw because they remove all the little discrepancies so easily. To my mind the drum sanding system is one of the most useful of its kind. However, there are many other types of sanding attachments for drills, and you will need to weigh up their cost against how long they might be expected to last.

Until recently only three hand-held sanding systems were available at a cost-effective price: the orbital, the belt and the disc sander. But this situation has changed, and now a variety of dedicated tools can be obtained at competitive prices and off the shelf. Additionally, improvements have been made to the original trio.

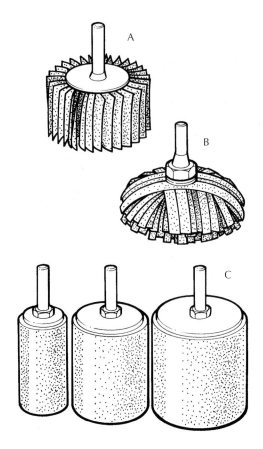

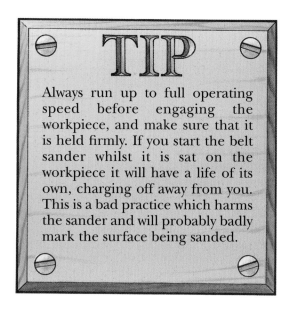

Fig. 130 *These sanders can be fitted into drills: a: straight flap; b: random flap; c: drum.*

TYPES OF SANDER

BELT SANDERS

I have a one of these and would not be without it – even though it can be vicious! The design of a belt sander is universal, and fairly straightforward. A fabric belt of sandpaper runs round two rollers, one of which is directly driven from the motor (Fig. 131a). The direction of rotation is clockwise, therefore the sander will tend to pull away from you. The free-wheeling roller is adjustable so that the belt can be centred, and this is important if you don't

TIP

Always run up to full operating speed before engaging the workpiece, and make sure that it is held firmly. If you start the belt sander whilst it is sat on the workpiece it will have a life of its own, charging off away from you. This is a bad practice which harms the sander and will probably badly mark the surface being sanded.

want it to come off, or to damage the body of the sander. It is also likely to be on a spring release mechanism that enables the belt to be loaded. Always check that the belt is fitted to go in the right direction; arrows will indicate this. Failure to do so reduces belt life and is also dangerous.

Heavy duty industrial belt sanders will have motors of 1000 watts or more, and are likely to be quite heavy; for general purpose use, anything from 500–750 watts will probably be adequate. Belt widths will vary; the two most common ones are 75mm and 100mm. It is better to have a wider width if possible, as you can do more with it. Naturally you will have to buy what you can afford – but do look at the cost of replacement belts before you buy. Some belt sanders have accessories that will make them more versatile. To avoid digging in, frames can be fitted that enable the sander to float (Fig. 132a); these can also be adjusted to ensure no excessive amounts of wood are taken off during the sanding process. Other accessories will allow you to fit the sander in a vertical position on the side of a

Fig. 131 Some powered sanders: a: belt; b: detail; c: mini belt of file.

bench, or to invert horizontally (Fig. 132b and c). These latter accessories are very useful, so check that your intended purchase can have this facility.

All in all, a belt sander in the workshop is a useful, but not essential, addition to the rest of the kit. If you need to remove waste quickly and efficiently, then go for one of these. Just be aware that the surface quality can be pretty rough if not used with care.

MINI BELT SANDERS

Some manufacturers call these 'power-files' (Fig. 131c). The one illustrated can be fitted with narrow belts of 6mm or 13mm; others are available with a variety of belt widths up to 50mm. Not an essential item, more of a novelty, but if you have an application, these small sanders can be used for a variety of jobs, not all with wood.

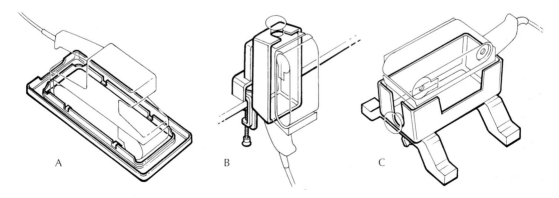

Fig. 132 Attachments for sanders: a: sanding frame for a belt sander; b: clamps to fix a belt sander in a vertical position, and c: horizontally.

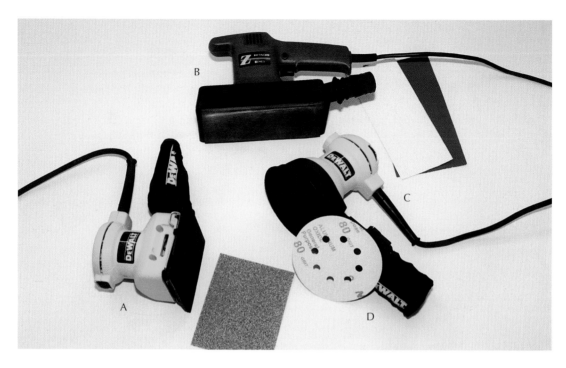

Fig. 133 Some of the smaller sanders and paper: a: palm orbital; b: two-handed orbital; c: palm random orbital; d: a sanding disc cut to help exhaust the waste.

DISC SANDERS

Disc sanders that simply rotate are not particularly useful in a woodworker's workshop because it is very difficult to get a satisfactory finish with them. On the odd occasions I have used one, they always seem to leave semi-circular marks all over the surface. I would not go out and buy one.

DETAIL (OR DELTA) SANDERS

Different manufacturers call these by alternate names. They are mini orbital sanders (Fig. 131b) that allow you to get right into those awkward, inaccessible corners never reached before! Most are lightweight with a fairly small motor, and they are not designed for constant, heavy use; for fine corner work they are excellent. Nor do they appear to leave any residual surface marking, which is a good

point. Some larger versions can change the shape of the sanding head to suit other applications. When considering purchase, try to estimate the amount of work the sander is likely to undertake; then buy the machine that best matches the workload.

RANDOM ORBIT SANDERS

I have only come across these tools recently and am very impressed by them. They come in various sizes and look similar to a disc sander (Fig. 133c), but have some significant operating differences. Similar to the orbital sanders, they run an elliptical, but random pattern; coupled with this is the circular rotation of the sanding disc. This arrangement is really effective in balling off the waste without marking the surface, and in circumstances where it is inappropriate to

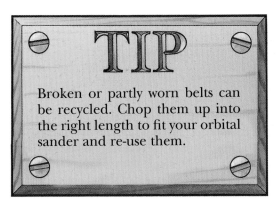

Broken or partly worn belts can be recycled. Chop them up into the right length to fit your orbital sander and re-use them.

use a belt sander but considerable work has to be done – these are the boys! Mine is a mid-sized model with a 300-watt motor and a 125mm disc size. Lighter- and heavier-weight models are available.

Most of these sanders will have an integrated dust removal system, whereby holes punched in the paper allow the dust to be sucked through the base pad and into a bag. It is important that the paper is positioned correctly to avoid blocking these exit holes. Next time I am looking for a finishing sander I will be tempted to buy one of the smaller versions available, the only slight caveat being the cost of the discs: because they are round they have to use a system that is self-fixing. However, the difference in cost between these discs and a roll of sandpaper needs to be taken into account when buying.

ORBITAL SANDERS

Often called a 'finishing sander', and every workshop should have one. Today they come in all sorts of different shapes and sizes (Fig. 133a and b). The pad is driven in tight elliptical patterns, sometimes with forward and sideways movement included. Some machines do have a tendency to leave small, swirling, circular marks on the finished surface, and to avoid this, choose one with a small

'orbit' because the smaller the movement the less noticeable any residual marking might be.

The orbital sander you choose will depend upon what you want to do with it. If you are only going to have one sander in the workshop then you might consider a mid- to large-range model. Anything with a motor over 200 watts probably drops into this category; the really serious tool goes up to 500 watts or more! This type of machine will be a two-hander, so check the vibration levels if you don't want to end up with tennis elbow or something similar. Palm sanders are smaller, and usually under the 200-watt motor size; they are more likely to be used for finishing off. If you have two, try and arrange things so that they both take the same paper width; this will save time and money. How the paper is retained is another important factor. I have come across some really awkward and weak systems in the past so check it out.

Like the random orbit sanders, some of the orbital sanders will have an integrated dust extraction system. I would avoid any that don't have a bag, as most of the dust will exit into the workplace. You can, of course, use plain paper without any holes, but the effect will be to create no extraction at all. In an ideal world you will use punched paper and hook up to an extraction unit. If not, wear a mask!

SANDPAPER

Throughout this book I have made the mistake of referring to 'sandpaper' when I should have been talking about 'abrasives'. As the correct name suggests, abrasives abrade, or wear away, the surfaces they are applied to. The rate of cut will be determined by the type of grain, the substance it is stuck to, and the condition or ability of the grain to cut.

Exerting extra pressure should have no effect at all. Cheap abrasives will be made from soft grain materials, they will have been set into a poor bonding material, and will clog easily.

Woodworkers will come across two main backing materials: paper and textile (Fig. 135a). The paper-backed abrasives come in a variety of grades: for hand-sanding applications, it is what is called 'A' weight; for use with a block, 'B'–'D' weight; and with power sanders 'D'–'E' weight. Sanding belts are made from textile to provide greater strength and flexibility; in

most cases this will be an 'X'-weight textile. 'J' is a very flexible textile back, often used in turning applications. In addition to the backing material there are, generally, two types of bonding adhesives used to stick the grain to the backing material: animal glues and/or resins. The animal or hide glues will soften in use, and are not really suitable for power tools. Resin, on the other hand, is more rigid and is ideal for them. Animal glues used in conjunction with a lightweight paper will give a softer cut as the grain flexes; this is desirable when hand finishing small profiles. Resin glue is hard; we have all tried to fold this paper cleanly, with little success! However, this hardness holds the grain firm and makes it ideal for power tool use.

To begin with, abrasive papers were manufactured with glass or sand stuck to them – hence glasspaper and sandpaper. The former is now found as a fine finishing paper – grade 00, flour paper – and the latter is no longer sand! There are three main grains used for sandpaper today. Garnet is crushed stone with better wearing qualities than glass; it is used for hand finishing. Aluminium oxide is tough and hard, and retains its shape under duress; it is therefore ideal for power tools. Third is silicon carbide, which is very hard. Today we tend to use the aluminium oxide papers, and perhaps the silicon carbide. The abrading process should be progressive, starting with a coarse grain and working down to a fine one. A final grain finishing paper of 240–320 will cover most of our needs (Fig. 135b).

CABINET SCRAPERS

Cabinet scrapers come in a variety of different shapes and forms (Fig. 136), and are used on hardwoods to produce a fine finish. Curly or interlocked grain timbers are difficult and impossible to plane, and these

Some sheet papers come cut to size and punched for power tool use. However, consider buying your abrasive paper in a roll and punching your own holes. Some sander manufacturers will supply a punch, or you can make one yourself (Fig. 134a and b).

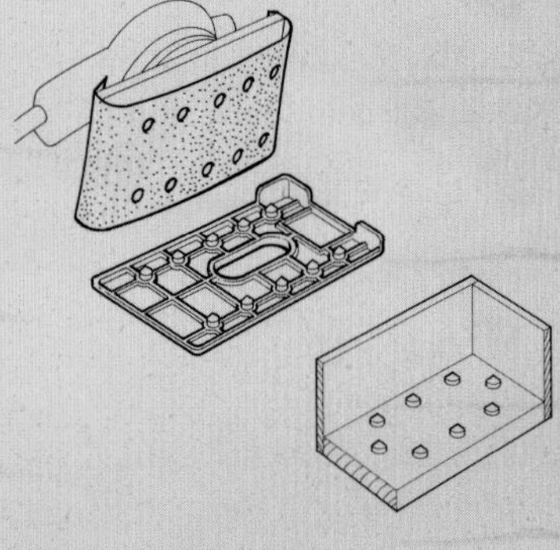

Fig. 134 Gadgets to punch holes in sandpaper are available: a: shop-bought; b: home-made.

Fig 135a Uses for paper- and textile-backed sandpaper

Weight	Material	Use
A	Paper	Light and flexible Handsanding
B	Paper	Slightly stiffer Hand and block
C	Paper	Medium stiffness Blocksanding
D	Paper	Medium weight Disc and orbital
E	Paper	Rigid Machine sanding
X	Textile	Medium Belt sanding
J	Textile	Light and flexible Ideal for lathwork

Fig 135b Sandpaper grit grades/sizes

	Silicon Carbide, Aliminium Oxide	Garnet	Glass
Very Fine	600		
Very Fine	500		
Very Fine	400	400 (10/0)	
Very Fine	360		
Very Fine	362	320 (9/0)	
Very Fine	280	280 (8/0)	
Very Fine	240	240 (7/0)	00 flour
Very Fine	220	220 (6/0)	0
Fine	180	180 (5/0)	
Fine	150	150 (4/0)	1
Fine	120	120 (3/0)	2
Medium	100	100 (2/0)	F2
Medium	80	80 (0)	
Medium	60	60 (1/2)	
Coarse	50	50 (1)	
Coarse	40	40 (1 1/2)	
Very Coarse	36	36 (2)	
Very Coarse	30	30 (2 1/2)	
Very Coarse	24	24 (3)	
Very Coarse	20	20 (3 1/2)	
Very Coarse	16	6 (4)	

For speed of paper changeover you might like to consider a Velcro, velour or self-adhesive system, whereby different grit sizes can be swapped over quickly without having to fiddle with catches and clips. Weigh up the cost in comparison to the convenience.

can be finished off most successfully with a good scraper. There are three steps to sharpening, or returning an edge, to a scraper: first, the original edge has to be filed flat; this is then polished using the edge of an oilstone; and finally, the edge is burred over with a 'burnishing' tool (Fig. 138a–c, overleaf). Scrapers are made from steel, and the burnisher has a round, smooth-faced rod of hardened steel. Shaped and curved scrapers may need a different approach to sharpening: the remaining burr needs to be worked off with a burnisher (Fig. 138d), and once the face is smooth, the burr can be restored in the usual fashion (Fig. 138c).

Scrapers can be difficult to use until you have mastered the technique. They should be pushed away from you, and tilted forwards slightly; very fine shavings will be produced, better than those from a smoothing plane if

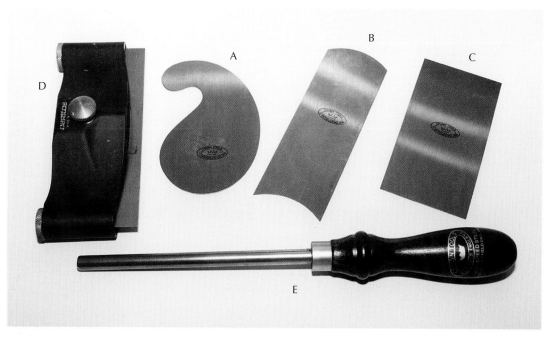

Fig. 136 Scrapers, etc.: a: curved; b: straight and curved; c: straight; d: straight adjustable holder; e: burnisher.

Fig. 137 A scraper plane attachment. (BriMarc Associates)

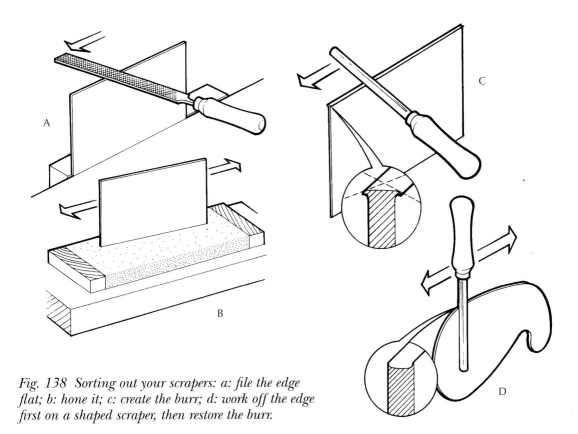

Fig. 138 Sorting out your scrapers: a: file the edge flat; b: hone it; c: create the burr; d: work off the edge first on a shaped scraper, then restore the burr.

you get it right. I must admit to finding the process a bit tedious, but there are some useful aids around to make it less so: for example, one manufacturer produces a holder whereby there is no need to apply thumb pressure (Fig. 136d). Tightening or loosening the centre nut increases or decreases the curve of the scraper; and there are other novel adaptations (Fig. 137). It is no problem to fit this scraper to a plane, and no doubt take some more of the tedium out of the work. You will, of course, still have to use a hand-held scraper to get into those tight corners!

TIP

Never buy cheap abrasives. Read carefully what it says on the packaging or in the brochure, and aim to buy the best you can afford. The cheaper papers will clog up and disintegrate quickly, and it is a false economy to buy them.

— 6 —

MARKING AND MEASURING

As before, all the tools are hammer- graded to indicate their level of desirability, in the opinion of the author, on a scale from one (the least) to five hammers (the most).

SQUARES

The marking out process for any project should only start after the timber to be used has been planed square; this can be achieved using hand or powered planes. Begin by planing one face flat, and this forms the first index point from which all other measurements and marks are taken. One edge is then squared off this face at right angles, and the try square is used to check this. Place the stock of the try square flat on the face, and slide it down until the blade rests on the edge (Fig. 139a); if it is out of square, gaps will be seen underneath it – and if so, re-plane or adjust the machine fence until it's right. As face and edge are worked flat, straight and square they should be marked in the traditional way to identify them (Fig. 139b). These two faces will then form the index points for the rest of that workpiece to be planed square to size. They will also form the basis for all subsequent markings around the piece (Fig. 139c).

Of course, none of this is any good if the try square is not true, and there is a simple way to check this. Using one straight edge on a piece of, say, ply, mark a line. Then reverse the square and mark again (Fig. 140a), and any slight discrepancies will show up. The same

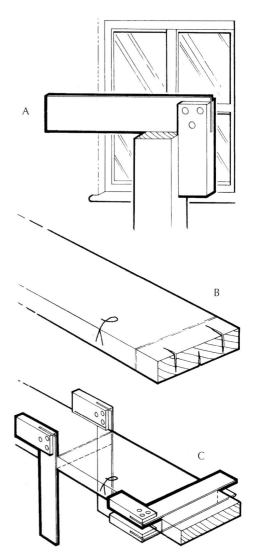

Fig. 139 Using a try square: a: to check the edge for square, hold it up to the light; b: mark the face and edge thus; c: using the marked faces as the index points from which to work.

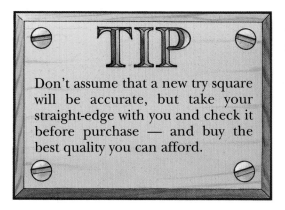

process should be repeated for the inside edge of the blade, to check that that is accurate too.

You also need to be consistent and use the right technique for making marks. The correct way is to angle the point of the marking knife, or pencil if you have to, in towards the square (Fig. 140b). If you consistently mark from the vertical

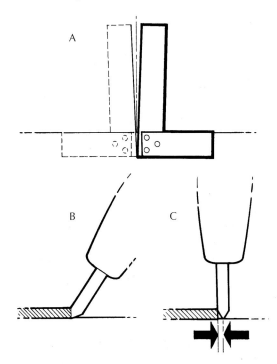

Fig. 140a: Check your try square for square;b: the correct way to mark out; and c: incorrect.

position (Fig. 140c), then the discrepancy will be multiplied on each subsequent face, and the result of this is that the marks never meet up! If you find your square is out of true, then you could either try to fix it, which might prove to be difficult, or you could dispose of it and buy a new one.

TYPES OF SQUARE

'Squares' is a relatively 'loose' term. Traditionally a number of other tools are broadly gathered together and described as squares.

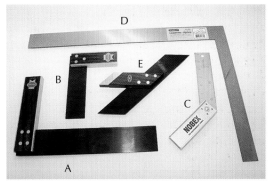

Fig. 141 A range of squares: a: large try; b: medium try; c: multi-purpose try; d: carpenter's square; e: mitre.

TRY SQUARES

There is a whole range of different try squares on the market, and traditional styles come in a variety of sizes (Figs. 141a, b and 142b). The largest I have seen was made by a cabinet maker for marking out sheet materials and table tops – a giant, with a blade over 24in (600mm) long; though I dare say there are bigger ones around somewhere. When working on a large piece I simply use a carpenter's square (Fig. 141d) in conjunction with my

Fig. 142 Some more squares and bevels: a: mini dovetail; b: mini try; c: sliding bevel with wing nut lock; d: ditto with lever lock; e: ditto with thumbnut lock; f: mini sliding bevel.

12in (300mm) try square for long squaring. It's always useful, if you can afford it, to have two or three different sized squares to hand; trying to mark out small stuff with a 12in (300mm) square is difficult! I have a 3in (75mm), a couple of 6in (150mm), and a 12in (300mm). Metal 'engineer's' squares are also available in a range of sizes. They are of all-metal construction, and some are solid; they are a useful addition to the range.

MULTI-PURPOSE SQUARES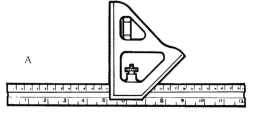

A number of multi-purpose squares are now available; probably the most common is the combination square (Fig. 143a), which combines the functions of a try square and a mitre square, a rule and a spirit level, and sometimes a small scratch awl is inserted into the main frame. Through the very nature of their construction they are less accurate, and

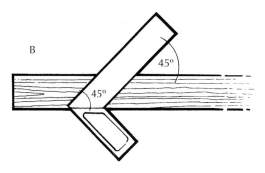

Fig. 143a: A combination square; b: some try squares are designed to be used as a mitre square also.

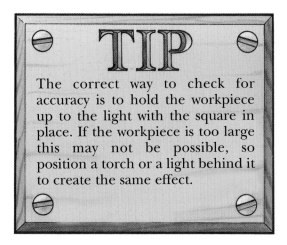

The correct way to check for accuracy is to hold the workpiece up to the light with the square in place. If the workpiece is too large this may not be possible, so position a torch or a light behind it to create the same effect.

the screw-tightening mechanism needs to work very efficiently at all times, because if it does not, the results will cause problems. I have one that I use often, but selectively. There is another multi-purpose square that can be set at various angles including 90 degrees (Fig. 141c); a spring mechanism in the stock clicks the blade into place.

MITRE SQUARES

As the name suggests, these squares are used to mark mitre angles at 45 degrees (Fig. 141e), and for marking out good, tight mitres they are essential, as long as they are accurate. Use the same procedures as with the try square to check

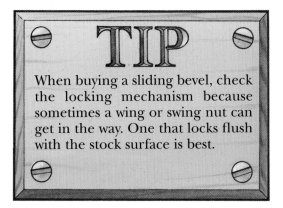

When buying a sliding bevel, check the locking mechanism because sometimes a wing or swing nut can get in the way. One that locks flush with the stock surface is best.

this: work off a straight edge, mark and then reverse the mitre square and mark again. With a protractor, check the accuracy between the two marks: it should be 90 degrees. Some try squares will have a 45 degree angle in-built into the stock that can be used to set a mitre (Fig. 143b). This is a useful extra, but it might not be quite so accurate in use as the purpose-made ones due to the shorter face contact.

DOVETAIL SQUARES

In these squares the blade is fixed, but offset at an angle from the stock, the degree of angle – known as the 'slope' – dictated by the type of dovetail; traditionally a softwood dovetail is considered to require a greater slope than a hardwood one, one-in-six as opposed to one-in-eight. The squares are generally fairly small and well made (Fig. 142a), and with care they will last a lifetime.

SLIDING BEVELS

Sliding bevels can be used to set a full spectrum of angles. The stock is split to accept the blade, which can be locked off into position (Fig. 142c, d, e and f); a 6in (150mm) or 8in (200mm) blade is probably about the most useful length. They are available in larger and smaller sizes – the model maker's sliding bevel illustrated (Fig. 142f) has only a 3in (75mm) blade. The main use for the sliding bevel is to set, and be able to repeat marks at predetermined angles. Further, it may be that an angle needs to be matched, in which case the bevel can be placed on a face edge, set, and locked, allowing the angle to be transferred to another workpiece.

The sliding bevel has other applications too, one of which is setting fences on

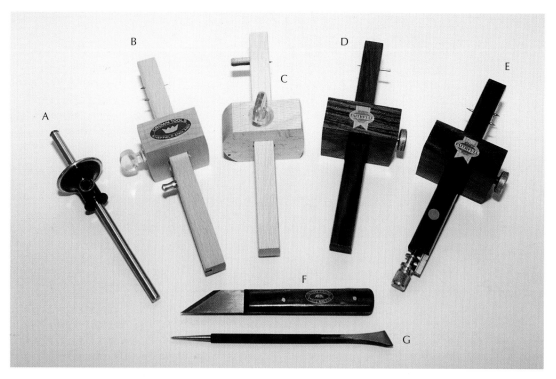

Fig. 144 Some marking gauges: a: beam; b: dual-purpose; c: cutting; d: traditional; e: dual-purpose fine-adjusting; f: a marking knife; g: combination marking knife and scratch awl.

powered saws and planing machines: after setting the desired angle, the stock is placed on the bed of the machine and brought up to the fence which is then adjusted. Boatbuilders and shipwrights have traditionally used them for marking out angles of decking and planking. With care, the sliding bevel can also be used to mark out dovetails.

MARKING TOOLS

Although I and countless others tend to use pencils for marking out, technically a marking knife will produce a more accurate result. In fact a hard pencil will mark clearly enough for most purposes; however, if a high degree of accuracy is required, then use the knife (though unfortunately if that is not used correctly,

the result will be similar!). The marking knife should be sharp, and angled into the blade against which it is going to run down (Fig. 140b). Knife cuts are traditionally called 'witness' marks; perhaps this is because, like a good witness, they are evidence of where you've gone wrong! The knife cuts do serve a purpose, especially with fine work, since used correctly, they sever the wood fibres, and this allows a much cleaner cut to be made with a saw or chisel.

MARKING KNIVES

Several types are available. Some are of a simple one-sided design (Fig. 144f) for left- or right-hand use; however, a double-sided knife with grinding angles of around 20 degrees is probably the best sort to have – though you can always modify a

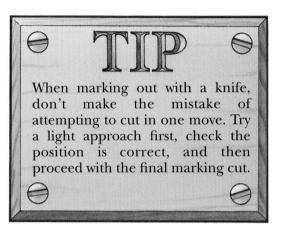

When marking out with a knife, don't make the mistake of attempting to cut in one move. Try a light approach first, check the position is correct, and then proceed with the final marking cut.

single-sided knife or buy a ready ground one (Fig. 144g). The one illustrated combines a marking knife at one end and a scratch awl at the other; this is quite useful, but it is a bit difficult to control because of the round shape. In fact you can always make a marking knife yourself! Use an old chisel, or one of those wide hacksaw blades – for the latter, cut it back and wrap some tape round for the handle; grind back the cutting edge and then hone it up until the desired edge is achieved. Or use a chisel instead!

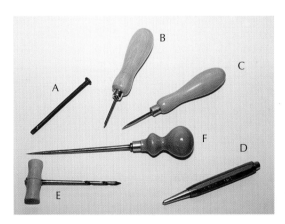

Fig. 145 Some odds and ends: a: an old 4in nail sharpened for marking; b: round bradawl; c: square bradawl; d: engineer's punch; e: gimlet; f: scratch awl.

SCRATCH AWL

Scratch awls can be used for marking wood, but proceed with care. They are best used with plastics and laminates (Figs. 144g and 145f). They cannot be classed as essential, but are nonetheless convenient to have in the workshop for occasional use.

ODDS AND ENDS

There are certain small marking and boring tools that you might find useful on occasions.

PUNCH

I often use a punch to mark the centre of a hole, especially when using a drill freehand. A simple engineer's punch (Fig. 145d) will cover most of your needs, particularly as it can be used on metal as well.

BRADAWL

These can be used for the same jobs as a punch; they come with round or square shanks (Fig. 145b and c). A bradawl has an additional use as a starting screw where a pilot hole is not necessary: simply twist it back and forth until a reasonable depression is made.

GIMLET

Like a bradawl, this can be used to create a pilot hole for a screw to follow. The difference is that it has an auger body that will remove waste as well. This facility means that you can bore deeper holes with it before starting your screw.

NAIL MARK

Basically this is a 4in (100mm) nail that has been ground and honed on both sides

(Fig. 145a); tapped lightly with a hammer it produces a simple mark. I use it for marking joint positions and numbers on the inside of components, and occasionally I might cut my initials into the underside of a finished project.

GAUGES

Gauges are used to mark down and across the grain; they produce a permanent mark, and should not be used carelessly on face materials. Generally they are made from wood, with plastic or metal locking screws. The beam, or stem, is usually slender and will have fixed or slide-adjustable pins, or spurs as they are occasionally called; the stock, or head, slides up the beam and is locked off at the appropriate position. The engineering sector has come up with some adaptations; the one illustrated (Fig. 144a) has a beam made from a steel rod with a special cutting disc at the top. Single or double pins should be made from hardened steel.

MARKING GAUGE

Simple marking gauges have only one pin (Figs. 144d and 146a). On a new gauge you might find that the pin is too long, so file some off or pull a bit back through the beam until it is at a comfortable length to use. Measuring between the pin, or disc, and the face of the stock sets the gauge; lock it off with the wing nut or screw. For fine adjustments lightly tap the head or the tail of the beam on your bench; no harm will come to the gauge, and it will move slightly each time you tap. If marking a middle line, check for centre by working off opposite faces: if the lines run down the centre they will fit exactly. One of these gauges can cover most of your needs in the workshop. For mortice-hole marking you

Fig. 146 Close-ups of: a: marking gauge; and b: cutting gauge.

will just have to use it twice! Across-the-grain marking can be a bit untidy sometimes, as the pin tends to tear out the fibres.

MORTICE GAUGE

When marking mortice holes it is useful to have two pins so as to be able to cut parallel holes simultaneously: one pin is permanently fixed, and the other is adjusted to suit the width of hole on a simple slide mechanism. Most mortice gauges will have a combination single and double pin action to make them more versatile (Fig. 144b and e). To use, first set the width of the pins for the mortice, or

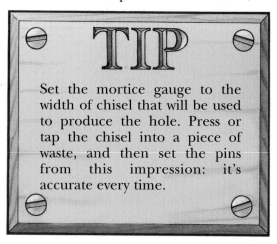

Set the mortice gauge to the width of chisel that will be used to produce the hole. Press or tap the chisel into a piece of waste, and then set the pins from this impression: it's accurate every time.

TIP

You don't have to have a marking gauge to run a quick line down the face or edge of a workpiece: in some cases your fingers will be good enough (Fig. 147a), or you could use a small block with a notch cut out of it (Fig. 147b).

If you wish to divide the width of something by an equal number, then use a rule offset at an angle (Fig. 147c); once the divisions have been identified, they can be marked down the length with a gauge.

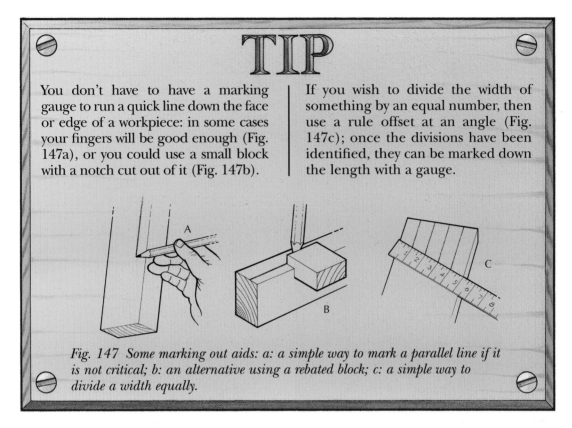

Fig. 147 Some marking out aids: a: a simple way to mark a parallel line if it is not critical; b: an alternative using a rebated block; c: a simple way to divide a width equally.

tenon; this can be done from a steel rule, or the end of the chisel that is to be used. Slide the stock up the beam to the appropriate setting, lightly mark, and check that the position is correct; use a bit of waste for this. Some mortice gauges can be adjusted by tapping head and tail like the marking gauge; others can't because of the fine adjustment screw.

CUTTING GAUGE

Rather than spending time sharpening the pins on your marking gauge, try adding a cutting gauge to your tool kit (Fig. 144c and 146b): it is specifically designed for marking across the grain because it cuts, rather than tears the fibres. It can also cut strips of veneer into strings for inlay work. Take care when exiting a cut, to avoid break-out; try

nicking the exit point first, then start the cut from the other end.

TAPES, RULES AND OTHER PARAPHERNALIA

There is an old saying: 'Measure twice and you only cut once', and how many times have we thought we knew what the measurement was, only to find the tenon was too small or the mortice too big? I know I have, so perhaps we should take heed of the common sense implied by this saying.

I am easily confused when people start talking metric, not because I don't understand, but because others try to make things more complicated than they need be. For instance, why do people talk about metres, centimetres and millimetres

TIP

Centre marking can be made easy with the following simple gadget (Fig. 148a): take up a piece of waste hardwood 6–7in (150–175mm) long; drill carefully, fitting two pieces of dowel and a pencil in the centre. Twist to make contact with the sides and hold there as you work down the length; it's always in the centre.

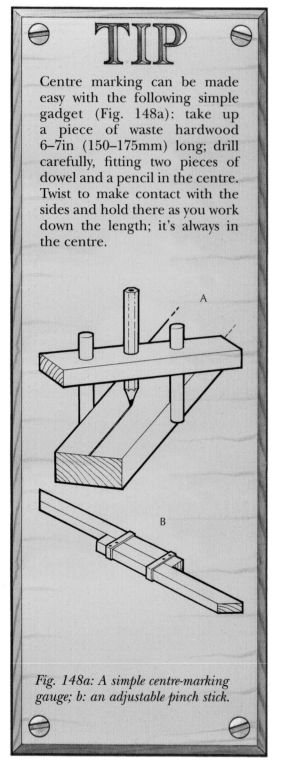

Fig. 148a: A simple centre-marking gauge; b: an adjustable pinch stick.

all in the same breath, when really it's all millimetres? Pick up a tape and look at it; certainly there are various highlighted marks, but the simple way to read it, and write it down, is in millimetres. For most of our general woodworking, increments of 1mm will be close enough; and if you really want to work in a smaller scale, then take a look at 1/32in and 1/64in; for some, that's going to be really confusing!

There are still those who use the whole length of the tape to measure between two points, and wonder why the outcome won't fit inside them. I have always taken great care of my tapes, yet the ends still get damaged. Of course it's supposed to be loose, though mine are always too loose, probably because I get too close to the bandsaw blade! In short, don't measure anything using the end of a tape or rule, because you'll most likely get it wrong. Use an index point, say at 4in (100mm), hold the tape on that, and mark off accordingly. One bit of advice: don't forget to add the 4in back on, or take it off, depending on what you are measuring.

It is highly advisable to draw out a full size plan of any projects that need some thought. I use an old sheet of MDF that has been painted over several times with a

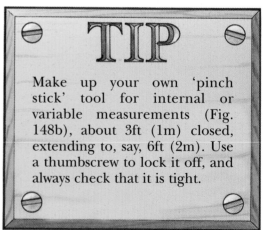

TIP

Make up your own 'pinch stick' tool for internal or variable measurements (Fig. 148b), about 3ft (1m) closed, extending to, say, 6ft (2m). Use a thumbscrew to lock it off, and always check that it is tight.

white emulsion. When making, say, a chair or bench, draw the front and side views – in fact just half of the front is quite acceptable, providing it is of symmetrical design. From the drawing you will get two main things: first, you will be able to see if the construction works, and looks all right. Second, you will be able to take measurements directly from the drawing onto your components; like this they should always fit! Transferring these measurements can be done with a tape or rule (bearing in mind what I have said about ends!), or use a measuring stick (sometimes called a 'story' pole); the stick is marked from the drawing and then laid on the component, and the measurement marked onto it. However, I am not convinced this is a good idea because the more times a measurement is transposed, the more likely it is to be wrong. Try it out and see what you think.

RETRACTABLE TAPES

For most measuring jobs in the workshop, one or two of these will be more than adequate: the range is huge, with all sorts of lengths and widths (Fig. 149b and c). Practically speaking, a 10ft (3m) tape is probably the most useful, and I can think of only a few occasions each year when I might need something longer; then a 26ft (8m) or a 33ft (10m) will cover just about everything. I actually have my father's old re-windable canvas tape, but it's not very accurate; there are steel versions available that are a lot better, but more expensive! Check the sliding tip of the tape, as most packaging allows you to pull that in and out; I know it will get damaged eventually, but at least start out with one that is square and straight. A blade that has both metric and imperial measurements will be most useful: although generally you will use one or the other, there will be times when you don't. Locking off

facilities are about standard, except for the cheap tapes; and if you want a spirit level incorporated, that's fine: you'll just pay a bit more for it.

METAL RULES

One of the other most important measures to have in the workshop is a steel rule. I have a few (Fig 149a and Fig 150a), of which I use regularly the 6in (150mm) and 12in (300mm). Unlike the tapes, they have imperial measurements marked on one face and metric on the other. For accurate work they are indispensable, they can also be used to calibrate and adjust various other bits of kit, and they are great as straight-edges as long as they are not damaged. They come in a variety of metals and finishes. I prefer the stainless or non-rusting steel rules, but light alloy ones are also available. For powered crosscuts, brass rules might be suitable (Fig.150d); these can be permanently fixed to the bench and indexed to the saw blade.

WOODEN RULES

In my humble opinion wooden rules are an inaccurate measure, too thick to use and often bent! Although they come in a variety of shapes and sizes, the longer, single piece ones are probably most useful (Fig. 150e). The folding ones always break and are useless for inside measurements, except for the one that has a sliding portion.

PLASTIC RULES

Plastic rules abound; probably the most useful ones are those that can be set at various angles (Fig. 149e). For everyday use, however, they will wear and lose their markings, so it may be best to keep them for the drawing board only.

STRAIGHT-EDGES

Purpose-made straight-edges (Fig. 150c) come in a variety of lengths; the one illustrated is 1m (3ft) long. These are very useful for some projects. If you decide to make one yourself, remember it needs to be both straight and flat.

SPIRIT LEVELS

You will need two of these, a short and a long one (Fig. 150b): the short one will fit into those awkward places, but may not be any use on wide-open faces. If the level is straight enough then you will also have an alternative straight-edge; two tools in one!

CALLIPERS

Engineer's callipers, or Vernier gauges (Fig. 149d) are occasionally useful for those exact measurements, internal, external or depth. If you are turning a lot, and or need to take inside and outside measurements, then a pair of simple callipers will suffice (Fig. 151f). The one illustrated is for external use: it is spring-loaded and has a fine thumbscrew adjustment; this type is probably more accurate than those which pivot on a single joint.

CIRCLE-MARKING TOOL

At some point you will want to mark out a circle. A simple carpenter's compass might do the trick (Fig. 151a), and is quite easy to make. However, there is a handy tool that can double up as a marking gauge (Fig. 151c): the rule section is 6in (150mm) long; the diameter is adjusted by sliding the pin up and down the metal rule; it's fixed in place with a thumbscrew. Trammel heads (Fig. 151b) are excellent for bigger circles because they can be fitted to any length of batten and adjusted to suit. It's quite easy to make your own. If

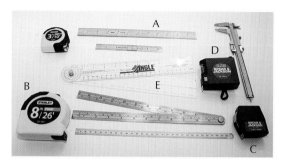

Fig. 149 A range of measuring kit: a: steel rule; b: a large retractable tape; c: basic retractable tape; d: Vernier gauge; e: adjustable plastic rule.

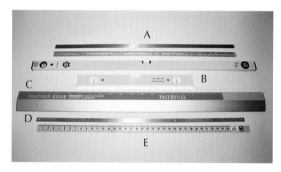

Fig. 150 Some larger measures and edges: a: steel rules; b: spirit levels; c: straight-edge; d: a brass rule for fitting to a workbench; e: a long wooden rule.

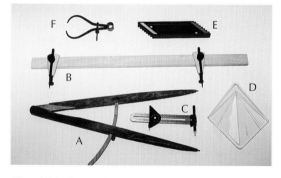

Fig. 151 Special measuring and marking kit: a: large carpenter's compass; b: adjustable trammel heads; c: adjustable combination steel rule; d: a plastic centre finder; e: height adjustment gauge; f: external callipers.

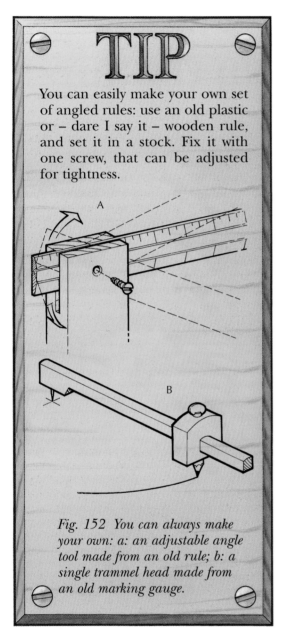

TIP

You can easily make your own set of angled rules: use an old plastic or – dare I say it – wooden rule, and set it in a stock. Fix it with one screw, that can be adjusted for tightness.

Fig. 152 You can always make your own: a: an adjustable angle tool made from an old rule; b: a single trammel head made from an old marking gauge.

you have an old stock from a marking gauge you're halfway there, if not, it's still easy to make one.

MORE ODDS AND ENDS

There are a great many gadgets for measuring, marking or gauging different things, and constant advertising from manufacturers to buy them. I have a simple plastic tool that enables me to find the centre of a dowel, or any turned item, and a square (Fig. 151d); by repetitive marking the centre soon becomes apparent. For lathe work it is great. Another little tool is a depth-setting gauge for my circular saw (Fig. 151e); this is placed on the bed of the saw and the blade raised or lowered. The stepped sides, which have imperial increments, allow for quick initial setting.

FOOTNOTE

Measuring and marking are critical parts of the construction process, therefore you should always try to have the right kit for the job. Some of the tools available are multi-purpose and therefore more cost-effective, but they may not save any time. As always, buy the best you can afford, and with luck they will last you a lifetime.

HOLDING AND FIXING

In this chapter we look at some of the different types of clamping and holding devices that are used, such as screws, nails and a few odds and ends. The hammer grading is only applied to the first section; for the rest you must set your own priorities.

CLAMPS

A number of short clamps are essential in any workshop, and you'll always want twice as many as you've got. When working on a limited budget it's probably best to go for a set of larger ones, say 6in (150mm); then you'll be able to cover the smaller jobs as well. All parts of the clamp that come into contact with your workpiece will need some sort of protection; I always keep the slim offcuts from tenon cheeks for this. Try to use a timber or ply that is softer that the material you are working on; if you don't, the pressure will probably mark the workpiece anyway.

Fig. 153 'G' clamps come in various shapes and sizes: a: heavy-duty; b: medium-weight; c: edge screw.

'G' CLAMPS

These clamps are immensely strong, and are essential for some jobs; probably the best size to have is 6in (150mm) between shoe and bottom jaw (see Fig. 153b). Larger versions, up to 12in (300mm) are available, as well as smaller ones, right down to the model maker's size at 3in (75mm). I find the best ones are those with a sliding 'tommy' bar, as illustrated, for tightening the thread. A couple of my older ones have wing nut-type heads, and I can't always get enough pressure on with them. Try to buy good quality clamps: a number of years ago I was tempted into buying some cheap imported ones, but I have broken all four of them, so in the long run they have turned out to be expensive. Look out for pointers such as 'drop forged' and 'ductile'; and if they are guaranteed, ask for how long.

A number of variations are available that will always be useful at times, but are not absolutely necessary for progress: for instance larger, heavy-duty ones – the one illustrated clearly shows a more substantial frame (Fig. 153a); clamps with a deeper throat which allow you to reach further into a joint; and the edge screw clamp –

TIP

Check the engineering when buying new or second-hand. This means winding the shoe right down to the bottom jaw and checking the alignment: they should match perfectly. If the shoe is slightly off at a tangent, then buy another one.

when securely fitted, pressure at right angles can be introduced. The one illustrated (Fig. 153c) can be adjusted along the frame of the clamp to locate exactly where you want it. If you can afford any of these, then add a couple to your range. However, these more elaborate versions are not essential; I manage without them – you will just have to be a bit more inventive at times.

SLIDING BAR CLAMPS

Sometimes called 'F' clamps because of their shape, a whole range of these is currently available – only a few are illustrated here (Fig. 154a, b and c). The basic principle is similar throughout: there is a fixed head at one end of a bar, and a movable one at the other, and you slide the one up and lock it off with a lever or through the tightening process. They are easy to manage if you need to work quickly or one-handed, the wide range of adjustments making them quite versatile. Depending upon the manufacturer, and of course the type and design, they come in different sizes: this can be anything between 4–5in (100–125mm) up to 5ft (1,500mm). The smaller ones can be used like a 'G' clamp and the larger ones instead of a sash cramp; in this latter instance they are better suited to light work. Look carefully at the shoes, as some of the lighter-weight clamps may be fitted with cork faces or soft plastic, in which case there will be no need for any further protection.

'SOLO' CLAMPS

I would always recommend these clamps (Fig. 154d). I bought my first pair a good ten years ago and they weren't particularly cheap even then, but they are still going strong! Based on a simple adaptation of a mastic gun mechanism they are light and

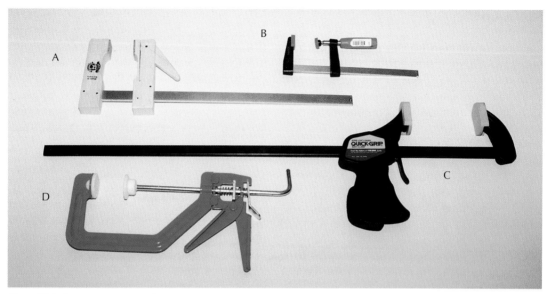

Fig. 154 Single-handed 'F' and 'G' clamps are available: a: cam; b: screw; c: quick grip; d: 'Solo'.

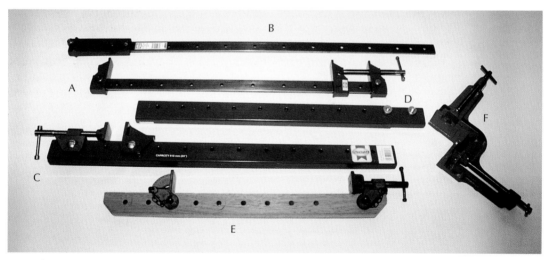

Fig. 155 This is a range of heavier duty cramps: a: sash; b: sash extension; c: box sash; d: box extension; e: cramp heads on wooden bar; f: mitre cramps.

easy to use, especially one-handed. For general purpose use these clamps are highly versatile and indisputably cost effective; in fact they are now cheap enough to consider having a number as a starter set. I have twelve in my workshop, and occasionally still have to use G clamps as well. A few, slightly different variations are obtainable. The most popular size is 6in (150mm), but I have seen some at 4in (100mm). A couple of things are worth checking: first, shoe fit – make sure it's true; and second, the grip – one of my old ones now slides when a lot of pressure is exerted on it. You shouldn't have this problem with new ones, but it's worth taking a look.

CRAMPS

A whole range of cramping systems is available to the woodworker today, some expensive and some not.

FLAT METAL 'SASH' CRAMPS

Of the various metal sash cramps currently in use, these are probably the easiest to handle and the most useful (Fig. 155a). Made up from a pre-drilled flat steel bar, the tail can slide up and be positioned close to the work to be cramped. Also, the pins that locate the tail can be spring-loaded, which is helpful. The threaded head usually has a tommy bar to tighten it. As with all methods of cramping, the workpiece will need to be protected against damage when under pressure. Sash cramps are used for general and heavy-duty work; they come in various lengths from 2ft (600mm) up to 6ft (1,800mm), with the option of extension bars (Fig. 155b). A couple of these at around 4ft (1,200mm) are essential in any workshop. Combined with other cramping methods, these can exert as much pressure as you will ever need.

'T'-BAR SASH CRAMPS

This is some really heavy-duty kit: instead of using a flat bar, a T-section is used, and like this the whole thing is strengthened and more rigid. The T-bar sash cramps will resist twisting and distortion under extreme pressure. They are usually slightly longer than the flat-bar ones, starting at 4ft (1,200mm) and going up to 7ft (2,100mm), with an extension bar option. These cramps are expensive and are unlikely to be used a great deal in a woodworking environment. Some would claim that if you need one of these to pull up a joint, then something is wrong!

TIP

To stop the pins dropping out, buy some 'R' clips from your local hardware store. Drill the appropriate sized hole in the tapered end, and fit the clip each time you adjust the tail end (Fig. 156a).

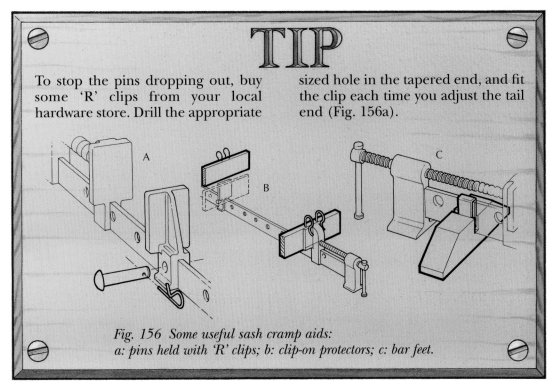

Fig. 156 Some useful sash cramp aids:
a: pins held with 'R' clips; b: clip-on protectors; c: bar feet.

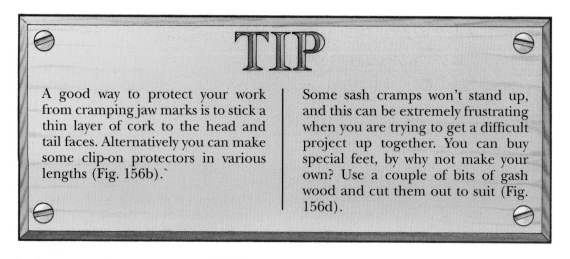

TIP

A good way to protect your work from cramping jaw marks is to stick a thin layer of cork to the head and tail faces. Alternatively you can make some clip-on protectors in various lengths (Fig. 156b).`

Some sash cramps won't stand up, and this can be extremely frustrating when you are trying to get a difficult project up together. You can buy special feet, by why not make your own? Use a couple of bits of gash wood and cut them out to suit (Fig. 156d).

BOX-SECTION SASH CRAMPS

These utilize a metal box-section instead of a flat or T-bar (Fig. 155c). Pre-drilled, and with movable head and tail, they are an alternative to the others. Once again, they generally have an extension bar (Fig. 155d), although they come in a slightly more limited range of lengths.

CRAMPING HEADS

This is one of the cheapest and most flexible ways to sort out your sash cramp requirements (Fig. 155e): instead of a steel box-section, a wooden bar is substituted. Cramping heads are available from several manufacturers; I have found the ones with a shorter thread to be best. Carefully hold the wooden bar to the gap and then drill at, say, 2in (50mm) centres; these holes need to be centred exactly on the appropriate head- or tail-locating holes, and be matched to the pin size. If you don't get all this right, the faces will cant back away from the positions in which you were hoping to exert pressure. I have enough pairs of these to cramp up most projects. I now also have various sets of wooden bars, usually in fours, pre-drilled from 2ft (600mm) to 8ft (2,400mm), which makes them really flexible – I have even used a bar that was 15ft (4,500mm) long! If you really have to, cramp initially

Fig. 157 Positioning sash cramps is important: a: packed out correctly; b: incorrectly. c: Use them to square up a frame.

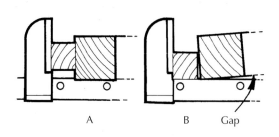

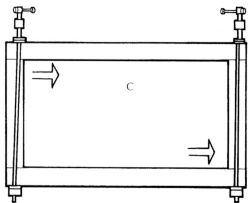

with a metal one, and then swap over to one of these; used carefully they are just as effective, and don't cost so much.

With all sash cramps, where you position the packing/protective pieces on the inside head and tail faces is important: correctly lined up, they should apply pressure directly to the joint (Fig. 157a); incorrectly aligned, and the joint may cant away (Fig. 157b). They can also be used to help when squaring up a frame, providing you have the joints in the right place! Cramp up the frame and measure across the inside diagonals: if the frame is square, these two measurements should be the same. If they are not, some slight adjustment may be needed, and to do this, you must offset the sash cramp one way or the other (Fig. 157c); once this manoeuvre has been carried out, it is most likely that the sash cramps can be returned to the correct position.

ODDS AND ENDS

Of the several alternative and specialist cramping tools and systems currently in circulation, each one needs to be evaluated and matched to your needs.

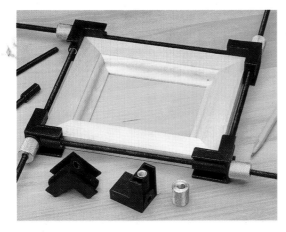

Fig. 158 Four-way speed frame cramp. (BriMarc Associates)

MITRE CRAMPS

Those who do a lot of mitring will be best served by a set of four of these cramps (Fig. 155f); the joint components are then simply slipped into each end of the cramp, located and tightened into place. With just one, each joint will have to be nailed up in turn. One of the simplest and most cost-effective mitre-cramping systems that I use is based on a pre-threaded bar (Fig. 158): a clever bit of engineering on the brass thumbscrew allows it to travel up the bar until it reaches the metal corner block. The whole is nearly self-squaring and is tightened by turning the nuts. Extension rods and joints are available to cramp large frames of up to about 4ft square (1,200mm).

PANEL CRAMPS

For jointing a lot of flat pieces for, say, table tops (Fig. 160): the design ensures that pressure is applied across the width whilst the whole lot is kept flat.

CARVING CRAMP

A bench-mounted cramping and vice system for carving (Fig. 161). This one can turn round and be tilted over, and if you want to work inside you can clamp it to a table top instead of a bench.

FLOORBOARD CRAMPS

A couple of these will prove invaluable if you have a lot of floorboards to lay (Fig. 162). As you extend and tighten the shoe against the wood a pair of jaws, on each lower side, dig into the joist – the tighter you go, the more grip you get!

SCREWS

Where do I start? There are so many options available today that it is often

TIP

You can make your own mitre-cramping system with some old bits of ply and some string! Glue some corner blocks onto a waste bit of ply and fit a substantial screw (Fig. 159). You will need four of these: position them at each corner, and tighten by twisting a waste strip across and around the string.

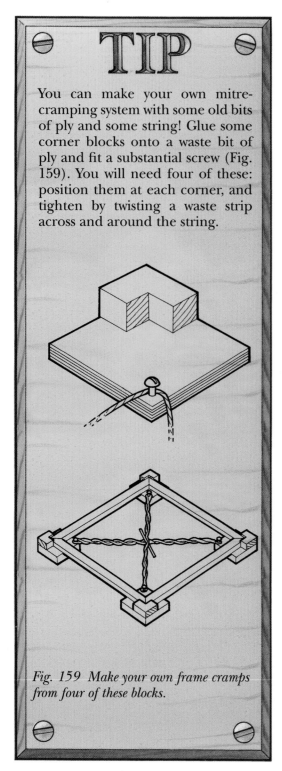

Fig. 159 Make your own frame cramps from four of these blocks.

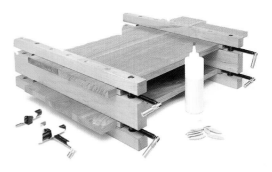

Fig. 160 A special panel cramp. (BriMarc Associates)

Fig. 161 An adjustable carver's cramp. (Record Hand Tools)

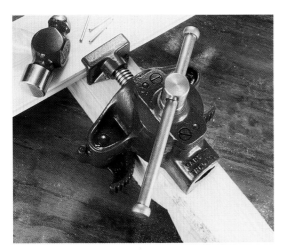

Fig. 162 Floorboard cramp. (Record Power Tools)

difficult to decide which screws to choose. This will not be a totally definitive work, but I shall attempt to describe the various uses typical for each screw type. (See Chapter 3 for the difference between slotted and cross-headed screws). Then it is up to you to select the systems that are best for you, and to go out and get the right equipment.

SCREW-HEAD DESIGN

There are three basic options regarding screw-head design: round, raised and countersunk (Fig. 163a, b and c); however, they can all be interchanged, and there are some variations on each theme. If you are going to leave a screw head exposed, then you might decide to use the round head or the raised head, as both can be fitted with screw cups; whereas for flush finishing work, the countersunk is ideal. And when I am using screws in a hidden location, I'll use anything! Providing they do the job, use whatever is to hand – I will recycle old screws under these circumstances!

SCREW-THREAD DESIGN

Threads have been modified and improved. A traditional wood screw has only a single cutting thread covering little over half its overall length (Fig. 163d); to use these correctly, each component to be jointed should be pre-drilled (Fig. 164a), particularly if trouble-free driving is required – and this practice is critical when working with most hardwoods. Double-threaded screws (Fig. 163e) are generally designed with a narrower shank that helps to avoid some splitting. They are particularly useful for work with fibreboards as they provide a greater surface area and thus grip. Also the pitch is likely to be steeper, which helps with the speed of insertions. A lot of the screws utilizing a double thread are designed to be used with power tools.

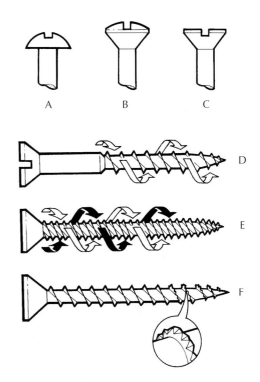

Fig. 163 Typical features of screws: a: round head; b: raised head; c: countersunk; d: single thread; e: double thread; f: serrated thread.

Another variation on modern thread design is the incorporation of a serrated edge to the first part of the screw (Fig. 163f). This apparently helps the screw to cut into the wood being jointed, and provides better grip with lighter materials. All these improvements in thread technology have had a beneficial effect on screws. However, some might find confusing the way in which the screw size is described: traditionally this was by gauge, but there has been a move towards metric. The chart opposite (Fig. 164b), should help clarify matters; it is a brief resume of some of the current screw designs. It's always important to pick the right screw for the job, so let's look at what is available.

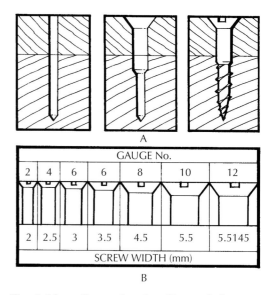

GAUGE No.						
2	4	6	6	8	10	12
2	2.5	3	3.5	4.5	5.5	5.5145
SCREW WIDTH (mm)						

B

Fig. 164 a Remember the pilot and clearance holes; b: a conversion scale from gauge to metric and vice versa.

TYPES OF SCREW

SOLID BRASS SCREWS

Available in a whole host of sizes with all the head variations (Fig. 165a, b and c), though in most cases they will still have a single slot to take a straight screwdriver. These will be used for face work where a brass screw will look a lot better than a steel one. They will not go rusty and,

unlike steel screws, they will not react with the high tannic acid content of woods such as oak and produce a stain. You should always pre-drill some pilot holes when working with brass screws, because they tend to overheat and will then break easily; to avoid this, first fit a steel one – this also saves the slot from damage. Beware of those brass-plated

TIP

To help traditional screws drive into the wood more easily, rub the end on a bar of soap or put a bit of grease on it; this will reduce friction, thus helping the driving process. It also makes it much easier to take them out again!

Another way to make driving screws easier is to spray some silicone furniture polish on them. Do this in the box to avoid making too much mess.

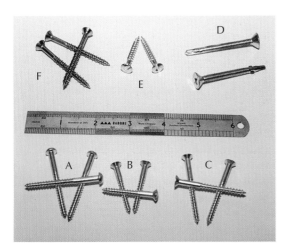

Fig. 165 A range of screws: a: brass round head; b: brass raised head; c: brass countersunk; d: timber to metal; e: security top; f: masonry.

screws claiming to be solid! One easy way to find out is with a magnet. They will rust through eventually, and are not worth the bother.

TRADITIONAL STEEL SCREWS

Most probably these will have a single slot head (Fig. 166d). For structural work they should be your first choice, especially if not assisted by glue. I use them for fitting buttons on table tops and suchlike; in these cases they are not on show but can be seen easily, and for traditional work such as I mainly do, they are just right.

ZINC-PLATED TWIN-THREADED SCREWS

One of the twin-threaded screws currently available (Fig. 166a); depending upon the wood density, these screws can be driven, quickly, straight into both hard- and softwoods. They are plated to help prevent corrosion, and hardened to help stop breakage. They are sold in imperial sizes with the shank defined by a gauge.

BLACK OXIDE, TWIN-THREAD DRYWALL SCREWS

Specially designed for fixing plaster boarding (Fig. 166f); they have an odd 'bugle' countersunk head design that can be set below the surface of the board without breaking the paper. The coating is to help reduce corrosion.

ZINC-PLATED SINGLE-THREAD SCREWS

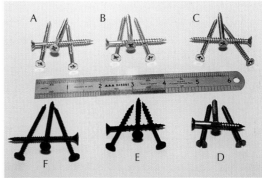

Fig. 166 More screws: a: zinc-plated twin-thread; b: zinc-plated single-thread; c: yellow zinc-plated single-thread; d: traditional wood; e: black oxide single-thread carcase; f: black oxide twin-thread drywall.

A general purpose wood screw (Fig. 166b); it has all the features of the twin thread, but can be driven a lot faster because of the wide, single thread. It also retains the imperial and gauge sizes.

YELLOW ZINC-PLATED SINGLE-THREAD SCREWS

A popular European screw (Fig. 166c). They are hardened, and have a sharp thread that cuts, rather than forces its way through the wood. In most woods and fibreboards there will be no need for a pilot hole, unless working near an end or edge. The shank is lubricated to ease entry.

BLACK OXIDE, SINGLE-THREAD CARCASE SCREWS

Similar in looks to the twin thread, this screw is designed for carcasing work with chipboard (Fig. 166e); even when driven into the edge of chipboard, these should hold.

TIMBER-TO-METAL SCREWS

A very specialist screw that avoids the need for pre-drilling in either the wood or the metal (Fig. 165d). It has a self-drilling point that bores through the wood first, and then goes on through the steel. The little lugs help make a clearance hole in the wood to avoid it lifting; they break off when they get to the steel.

SECURITY SCREWS

Designed to be put in, but not taken out! The head has a one-way 'clutch' slot (Fig. 165e), and a straight screwdriver is used to drive them home.

MASONRY SCREWS

With a specially designed, serrated thread, these screws don't need plugs or anchors (Fig. 165f). The object to be fixed is pre-drilled, and a small pilot hole driven in the masonry, of a size to suit the screw being used. The hardened screw-thread serrations can then be passed through and driven straight into the concrete.

COACH SCREWS

Suitable for those tough, maybe outdoor jobs (Fig. 167c): a cross between a screw and a bolt, these usually come in standard metric sizes from about 25mm long with a 6mm diameter, M6, up to160mm x M10. There is generally a choice between zinc-coated or steel. A clearance hole is required in the first component and a pilot hole in the second. Use a washer under the head to help with the final turning.

COACH BOLTS AND NUTS

Occasionally used by woodworkers (Fig. 167a), these are another fixing for anything that needs to be really secure; an added advantage is that they can be undone as well. As standard they are manufactured with a fully threaded or partly threaded shank. If you use the latter, make sure that enough thread will be exposed to tighten the joint, and allow for some sinking into the wood. Sizes range from 30mm long x M6 up to 180mm long x M10. Your hardware supplier may have these in steel, or zinc-coated, or with a painted finish: you will have to choose the right one for the job in hand. These bolts are designed not to turn in the wood: once the square under the head is forced into the top component, it locks and will not move. One of the best ways to engage this lock quickly is to push the bolt as far in as possible and then give the head a whack with a hammer! This forces the square into the wood and takes up any slack. Like with the coach screw, it's a good idea to use a washer, though under the nut this time. To avoid joint slippage, consider using pronged 'T's with these bolts (Fig. 167b); those illustrated are single-sided and should be sufficient for most holding jobs. Different designs with prongs on both sides are available.

THREADED RODS

For really long fixing. Standard sizes are metric again with, usually, a fixed length of 300mm or 1,000mm, diameters from M4 to M12. Use these in a similar way to the bolts, but with two nuts, but take care that the rods don't turn in the holes because there is no square head to lock

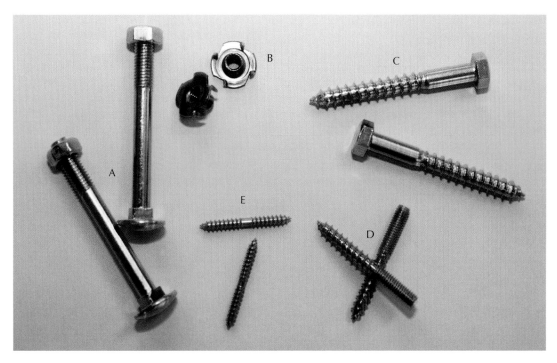

Fig. 167 Some odds and ends: a: coach bolts; b: spiked connectors; c: coach screws; d: dowel screw with thread one end; e: dowel screws.

them off. Zinc-plated rods should be considered in preference to plain steel, depending upon the application.

DOWEL SCREWS

There are two types of these: the first has a screw thread on one end and a bolt thread on the other; the second has screw threads on both ends (Fig. 167d and e). The screw and bolt arrangement is used when a threaded bolt needs to protrude from a surface onto which another component can be fixed. They are often fitted to tables where the legs need to come off for storage. The double screw-threaded one is used when a blind fixing is required: the first component has the screw inserted, with fixed jaw pliers, and the second component is then attached. Both types of screw come in a small range of sizes, in metric and imperial.

NAILS AND OTHER SPIKES

Nails have come a long way from the first blacksmith-cut and forged nails that were once the norm. In this section I have tried to include the majority of hammer-driven fixings you are likely to come across, but there are many more! Industrial power tools are available that provide a range of specialist fixings – wood to metal, wood to concrete and so on – so it is worth calling at your local tool hire shop to see if that difficult job can be done more easily with some help. Air- and gas-operated nailers were discussed in Chapter 1, and as prices come down, these tools are becoming more accessible to the general woodworker. However, you may find them restricting in that there is no 'universal' tool – you have to choose between a tool that fires nails, another that fires pins, and yet another staples. They may be a lot quicker under certain circumstances, but are not always very flexible. In the meantime let's take a look at those you generally have to strike with a hammer.

ROUND WIRE NAILS

Made from lengths of round wire with a simple forged, flat head and a point (Fig. 168a). This is probably the most common nail used for general carpentry; it also comes in a wide range of sizes and shapes. Standard wire nails are now generally supplied in metric sizes, from 25mm long x 1.8mm, up to 150mm x 6mm. They may be 'bright', which is plain steel, or possibly have a galvanized coat. Round wire nails can be drawn out with the right tool. A variation that is designed to hold firmer is the annular ring nail (Fig. 168b): also available in a variety of sizes, the rings applied to the shaft provide more grip and resist removal; when pulled they tend to tear the wood.

SPECIAL WIRE NAILS

These also come in all sorts of shapes and sizes; illustrated is a 'clout' nail with a large head (Fig. 168c), used for fixing roof tiles and slates. Some are made with extra-large heads. A 'felt' nail is similar to this, but has an even larger head to prevent it cutting through the felt that it is fixing. Plasterboard nails are like a standard wire, but have a jagged shaft for extra purchase, especially important when fixing ceilings. One more for this group, although it should not really be here, is the square twist nail (Fig. 169b); like the ring shank nail, these are specially designed to resist extraction – they twist when driven in, and twist when pulled out. They are usually only available in a very limited range of sizes.

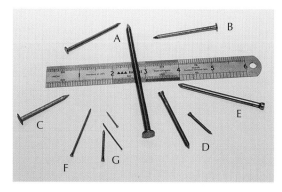

Fig. 168 Common nails: a: round wire; b: round annular ring; c: clout; d: oval; e: lost head; f: panel pins; g: veneer pin.

OVAL NAILS

Oval in shape, these are designed to be used close to the end of the timber being jointed (Fig. 168d); the elongated shape should run with the grain, and not across it. The theory is that the slimmer body does not exert too much sideways pressure on the fibres, thus avoiding any splits. The head is designed for full penetration: if you are good enough they can be hammered flush with the surface; most of us, however, will need to use a punch to tap them away. They are available in bright or galvanized steel finishes. The range of sizes is limited to the type of application.

LOST-HEAD NAILS

Used for the same sort of jobs as the oval. It has a round wire shaft with a slightly flared head (Fig. 168e). The name comes from the usual practice of punching the head below the surface it is fixing; if necessary, the hole is filled to finish off. This nail is often used on floorboards, where it is entered at an angle, driven flush home, and then punched away.

PANEL PINS

A smaller and slimmer version of the lost-head (Fig. 168f), these are used where a light fixing is appropriate for attaching, say, a beading onto a panel. They are driven near to the surface and then punched away. The small hole can sometimes be left, but is tidier filled. Sizes range from about 12mm to 40mm long, with shafts about 1.5mm.

VENEER PINS

An even slimmer version of the panel pin and used in similar application (Fig. 168g), these are really lightweight nails that will bend very easily; left flush with the surface they are not really visible. The theory is that because they are so small, no filler is needed; when painted over, the slight recess will be filled (personally I still fill them). Sizes are usually available similar to the panel pin but with a 1mm shaft diameter.

BRASS PINS

A number of these can be found (Fig. 169d). Those that look like panel pins should be used where staining may occur, or when a brass head may be part of the overall design. The larger-headed ones are used to fit escutcheons and other brass fittings. The best procedure is to tap them in nearly flush, and finish off with a punch.

'ROSE'-HEADED NAILS

These are an expensively forged, traditional nail (Fig. 169a); many of the old-fashioned nails used to look like this, each one individually made. Take a close look at any ancient door, say in your local church, and you should see some of these. They are only available in limited sizes. They should be hammered in with the head exposed, and are really for decoration and reproduction; the cost will stop you using them for anything else!

CUT NAILS

Another traditional nail (Fig. 169c); punched out of a flat sheet, they are available in two or three sizes, and might be used when making, say, a traditional-style ledge and braced door. The nail is driven through and then bent over and returned. Before the advent of nail guns they were used a lot in the building trade to fix skirting boards directly to the

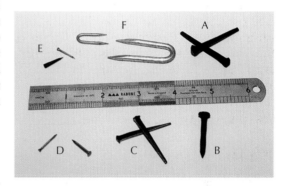

Fig. 169 A few more: a: rose-head; b: square twisted; c: cut; d: brass pins; e: brads; f: staples.

masonry – a particularly crude practice that usually resulted in the skirting board coming loose.

BRADS

Designed for glazing use only (Fig. 169e), there are two types: the flat one is produced in the same way as a cut nail, from a flat sheet, the square one is like a panel pin. Because the faces are flat they can be run up tight to the glass without breaking it.

STAPLES

These come in a wide range of sizes and are usually galvanized (Fig. 169f). The large ones are used around the farm and garden for fixing fence wire and suchlike; and the upholstery trade traditionally used quite a lot of the small ones as anchor points for string etc. Take care when knocking them in, as the hammerhead can easily slip and get your fingers!

MORE ODDS AND ENDS

There are a number of other ways to joint wood, some visible, some not, and some which need help to be made invisible.

PLUG CUTTERS

One of these will be helpful for those instances when you would like to conceal a screw or a nail (Fig. 170a). They are used in conjunction with a matching bit that drills the recessed hole (Fig. 170b). The fixing is then inserted and driven home, and a plug is cut from a similar piece of timber (Fig. 170c), glued and taped into place over the fixing. Later, when the glue has gone off, the plug is cleaned off flush with the surface. The best plug cutters are those that produce a tapered side; these will always create a tight fit when used with the correct drill bit.

Fig. 170 A range of different fixings: a: plug cutter; b: matching bit; c: plug; d: corrugated fasteners; e: star dowels; f: ribbed dowel; g: home-made dowel; h: dowels cut from long lengths; i: beech biscuits.

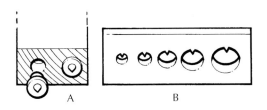

Fig. 171a Dowel centring spikes; b: home-made metal dowel maker.

CORRUGATED FASTENER

Designed to be hammered across joints to provide extra strength (Fig. 170d): made from corrugated steel with a sharpened leading edge, they are positioned centrally and at right angles to the joint. The design of the corrugations tends to draw the joint together as it is hammered home. For rough carcasing and, say, trellis work they are ideal.

STAR DOWELS

A metal, pointed and barbed dowel (Fig. 170e); in softer woods these can be driven straight into a joint. Typically they are used to lock in place mortice and tenon joints. They are available in two or three sizes.

RIBBED WOODEN DOWELS

Also typically used for securing or making a joint (Fig. 170f): a lot of modern furniture uses these dowels in the butt joints. The ribs allow excess glue to escape past the body of the dowel; if too much glue is used and can't escape, the dowel won't seat properly. There are various aids available to help line up the dowel holes (Fig. 171a); in this case the first hole is drilled and the aid inserted. The second component is brought up to, and pressed against the spike that then marks the centre for the matching hole. In the right application these dowels are very useful; however, I personally don't like using them in furniture making.

HOME-MADE SHORT DOWELS

The basis of a home-made dowel is a metal bar with a matching-sized hole drilled into it. Cut your wood square, slightly oversize, point one end and drive it through with a hammer. The result is a fairly rough dowel (Fig. 170g), but they will do the job in most cases. If you intend to produce any number of these, have a dowel plate made up (Fig. 171b). The spike on the side of each hole on the plate produces a groove to relieve the glue.

DOWELLING RODS

Another cheap way to make your own dowels is to cut down lengths of standard-sized dowel (Fig. 170h). Create a relief cut for the glue by sawing down one side.

BISCUITS

Also known as 'flat dowels' (Fig. 170i), these are used in conjunction with a biscuit jointer (Fig. 3), discussed briefly in Chapter 1. Biscuits are available in various sizes to suit most applications. They are probably best used for jointing tops, but they can also work in other joint locations. Remember always to keep them in a warm, dry place – they are supposed to expand after they have been inserted in the joint!

ADHESIVES

Before we discuss the main subject of adhesives, a couple of 'specials' should be mentioned. Various suppliers will stock an adhesive in a tube that can, in some cases, do away with the need for any other type of fixing (Fig. 172a). It is not suitable for use on high quality reproduction furniture, but is ideal for fixing skirting, architrave, wall cladding and suchlike. Obviously the surfaces to be joined need to be clean and sound. This adhesive offers a viable alternative to traditional fixing methods; it can bond wood, masonry and metal in any combination, and sets very quickly. If you have ever watched a carpet being laid, this is the stuff that is applied to fix those awkward bits of gripper! It is well worth considering for all sorts of jobs.

The second one is expanding foam, which might be suitable for 'second fix' tasks. The foam comes in tubes, and the cheapest way to use it is with the dispensable nozzle that is supplied with it (Fig. 172b). Because the foam reacts when exposed, these simple nozzles tend to clog up quickly; if you want to re-use the tube then you'll need a supply of them. If, however, you are likely to use foam a lot, then consider buying an applicator gun that can be purged with the right cleaner. The foam expands to something like thirty times its liquid state in size, so take care where you use it, and make sure there is somewhere behind the joint for the excess to go. Cleaning up after it has hardened is not a problem, but you'll probably need a knife of some sort (Fig. 172c). I have successfully fixed door linings and other frames with expanding foam where traditional fitting techniques have been limited or non-existent. It has additional benefits as a gap filler, for heat,

Fig. 172 Alternative fixers a: adhesive tube; b: expanding foam; c: a range of craft knives.

and as a partial sound insulator.

Whenever we use one of the wide range of glues available we should be aware that the bonding process has two parts to it. The first is the adhesive's ability to penetrate the wood structure of the

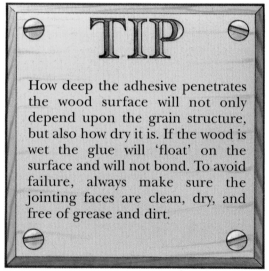

TIP

How deep the adhesive penetrates the wood surface will not only depend upon the grain structure, but also how dry it is. If the wood is wet the glue will 'float' on the surface and will not bond. To avoid failure, always make sure the jointing faces are clean, dry, and free of grease and dirt.

components being joined; this mechanical part of the process will form small 'keys' into the adjacent faces. The second part is its strength in actually sticking to the wood itself. In combination, and with all the right conditions applying, the resulting bonds should be stronger than the materials they are joining. A number of quite different

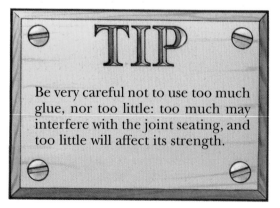

TIP

Be very careful not to use too much glue, nor too little: too much may interfere with the joint seating, and too little will affect its strength.

Fig. 173 Table showing the properties and uses of different adhesives.

	Water resistance	Rigidity	Curing time	Dry colour	Gap filling
Animal glues	poor	excellent	6 hours	brown	poor
PVA Adhesives	poor	poor	2 hours	clear	poor
Cascamite	excellent	excellent	8 hours	cloudy	good
Epoxy Resin	excellent	excellent	30 hours	clear	excellent
Contact Adhesive	excellent	poor	20 mins.	cloudy	poor

adhesives are available on the market, but I shall focus only on those that are generally available; I have also prepared a rough guide to each of those described (Fig. 173).

ANIMAL GLUES

The most common of these is hide or 'scotch' glue, made from boiling up cattle parts such as horns and hooves. This is the furniture maker's traditional glue. Granules or powder are heated and dissolved in water using a special kettle. Liquid animal glues are also available for those who don't want to bother with this. The glue is easy to apply, and a reasonable length of time can elapse before it goes off, a useful attribute when fixing a complicated structure or one with many joints. It has the added advantage of being reversible, in that applying a warm iron and a little water will loosen most joints enough to part them. Scotch glue is one of the favourites for fixing veneers. Its flexibility and longer setting time give you the opportunity to manipulate the veneer into the right position before it 'goes off'.

Make sure that both the veneer itself and the sub-frame work are thoroughly dry before application to avoid any 'telegraphing' – joint shrinkage that might become apparent later. This is a useful glue for the right applications if you want to replicate traditional methods.

POLY VINYL ACETATES (PVA) ADHESIVES

Another water-based glue: particles of PVA are suspended in water, and when the water evaporates the bond is formed. They are commonly available for both interior and exterior use. They never fully harden and should not be used where a rigid joint is required, such as a table top, where it might 'creep'; they are more suitable for framework, when at times a slightly flexible joint is more desirable. The drying time depends upon the local temperature, but will normally be long enough to put together complicated structures. Some rapid drying versions are available which are useful when gluing a series of components together in a particular order; to really speed up the curing process, use commercial radio frequency (RF) machines and tools. PVA dries clear and fairly hard. Non-waterproof versions will appear to cloud up and loosen if they get wet.

UREA FORMALDEHYDE RESIN (UFR) ADHESIVES

The most easily recognizable of these is 'cascamite': this is a trade name for the white powdered resin and hardener that can be purchased in various sized containers. The powder is mixed with cold water, which releases the hardeners. It should be stirred until a thickish, creamy result is achieved; if it is too stiff it will go off rapidly, and if too thin the bonding qualities will be affected. Never use warm water, because this will turn the whole lot into putty and harden within minutes! Cascamite curing time is directly related to the temperature prevailing when it is applied, so bear this in mind when gluing up: for instance in summer, for best results it might pay to get up early in the morning when conditions are cooler; and when it is cold, cramped-up joints should be left longer to ensure they have cured correctly. This glue forms a rigid joint and is ideal for structural use. It dries into a glass-like substance that can be cut or planed. Beware of face surface contact, however, especially when staining, because residual glue will seal the grain completely and stop stains penetrating the wood; this leads to a light tidemark around joints.

EPOXY RESIN ADHESIVES

These come in a two-part kits. Hardener and resin are mixed together before application, and some testing may be necessary to see how much time you have before the joint becomes inflexible; this is especially important with larger projects. Be careful, and follow the manufacturer's mixing instructions: failure to do so might result in joint failure. The chemical reaction between resin and hardener creates heat and is fairly rapid. This is an ideal glue for waterproof joints in exposed locations; because of this it is often used by boat builders and in other coastal work applications.

CONTACT ADHESIVES

Most contact adhesives are designed to allow different types of material to be bonded: you spread both joining surfaces with the adhesive, wait a pre-determined time, then press the two together. Typically laminates may be fixed to a substructure, for worktops, or materials such as leather and plastics may be fixed to wood, metal or masonry. Keep an eye on these adhesives once you have applied them, because they may start setting more quickly than you anticipate; the best type to use may be those that have a time delay mechanism incorporated within their structure, because this allows a certain amount of manoeuvrability before they finally bond the two parts together. Contact adhesives are not ideal for structural wood-to-wood jointing, because their rubberized base allows too much slippage to take place.

— 8 —

SHARPENING AND SETTING

If you are planing, cutting, or using a router, then at some point you will probably want to sharpen or touch up a cutting edge; and unless you have a full set of hardpoint saws, these will need some attention as well. Of course, someone else can do this for you if you don't want the job and can afford to pay them to do it; however, the best policy is to try and protect all cutting edges as a matter of routine, and thus avoid having to sharpen them too often.

Depending upon the type of edge to be sharpened, you will probably need a range of files, stones and a grinding wheel. The files will be specific to the job, although a set of small files will always be useful. Stones are used to hone the final edge, and grinders to create the basic angles. Always buy the best you can afford, look after them, and they will give you good service. Various options are available; the most common are described below.

OILSTONES

Originally made from a natural 'Arkansas' stone, oilstones can be man-made from silicone carbide or aluminium oxide. These are probably the most common of the stones found in workshops. The range of grit size is quite good, and they are available as individual stones. A favourite policy is to have two bonded together in, say, fine and medium or medium and coarse combinations. Make up a box in which to house the stones (Fig. 174a), and flip them over when changing grit size.

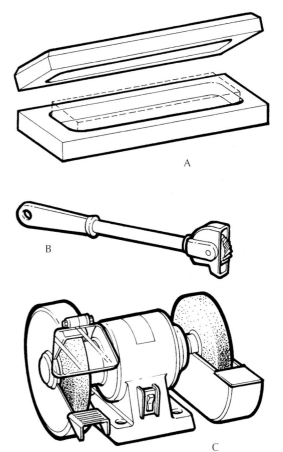

Fig. 174 a: Oilstone box; b: grinding wheel dressers; c: combination dry and wet stone grinder.

Beware of creating hollows as time goes on, as these are difficult to get rid of; be sure to sharpen over the whole face of the stone. Some small stones are available for sharpening shaped cutters.

157

WATERSTONES

A waterstone should be soaked before use, and should never have oil applied to it. These stones can be made from both natural and synthetic materials, and have an extremely large range of grit sizes. They work and cut quickly; at the extreme end they are probably the stones that can produce the finest finish. Make a box for these as well; when this is positioned and tightened into a vice it will hold the stone firm enough for you to work on it.

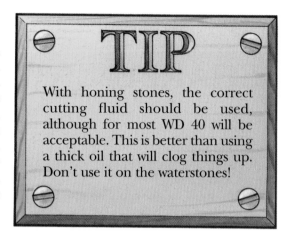

With honing stones, the correct cutting fluid should be used, although for most WD 40 will be acceptable. This is better than using a thick oil that will clog things up. Don't use it on the waterstones!

DIAMOND STONES

These are quite expensive but will last for a long time, probably longer than you! Extremely hard, they are easily capable of sharpening TCT router cutters and are therefore very useful. The cutting surface is made up in a grid or chequered pattern and is bonded to a plastic base. They can be purchased with a wide range of grit sizes, and are used in the same way as the oil- and waterstones. Small, individually shaped diamond stones are also available for sorting out those router cutters.

DRY STONE GRINDERS

When we talk about grinders we are probably thinking of one of these. They can be single- or doubled-ended, and take wheels made from various abrasive materials. With a double-ended machine you may wish to have a coarse, quick-cutting wheel on the one end, and a finer wheel on the other. Take care when using these wheels because they can easily overheat the cutting edge, and if this happens, its ability to keep an edge or to resist chipping may be affected. I always keep a container of cold water to hand, and cool the blade off before it gets too hot. Also take care that the face of the wheel does not become rounded: this

would make straight grinding all but impossible. The wheels can be straightened using a 'star' dressing tool (Fig. 174b): this dresses the surface of the wheel by moving it from side to side, and restores the flat surface. It will cut some of the wheel away, thus reducing its size; however, it will also get rid of anything that might have clogged the surface. Take care to ensure that too much pressure is not applied when doing this.

WET STONE GRINDERS

With one of these, the problem of the cutting edge overheating will not arise. The wheels are mounted vertically or horizontally, and either run in a trough of water or have a drip feed from above; the wheel surface is therefore continuously drenched with water, thus keeping the whole lot cool. The grit range is wide and quite fine; some tools can be used straightaway, without further honing.

Combination machines (Fig. 174c) have a high-speed wheel at one end and a waterstone wheel at the other, and for most grinders there will be a range of additional fittings that can be added to help with the process. Some will be suitable for narrow blades (Fig. 175), and simply hold the tool at the right

Fig. 175 Swivel attachment for a wet grinder. (BriMarc Associates)

angle. Grinding wider edges sometimes causes problems because it is difficult to keep them straight. Attachments are available to help with this if you are not confident enough to do it (Fig. 176). Always wear safety glasses, goggles or a face shield when using a grinder; it'll keep you safe and cut down the waiting list for the rest of us!

SHARPENING DRILL BITS

Drill bits are often damaged – sometimes when they get dropped or driven into a nail! Very often a set of small files will probably be more than sufficient to restore an edge; you'll probably need a range of sizes and cuts. Coarse cuts will be needed when a large imperfection has to be filed out, and a fine one for touching up. Some of the small diamond stones will also be useful, especially for sharpening any bits with wings – if the wings aren't sharp enough they will produce a poor edge to the hole.

Auger and spur bits should be sharpened from the original angles (Fig. 177a and b), and they will have to be done by hand unless you have a special wheel for your grinder. Some of the adapted **dowel bits** can be sharpened quite simply on a grinding wheel, as long as you have a square corner to fit (Fig 177c). **Forstner bits** can be problematic, because getting the right curve to the edge on the inside is difficult unless you have a cone-shaped grinding wheel. Fortunately most of these can be taken apart, making the different

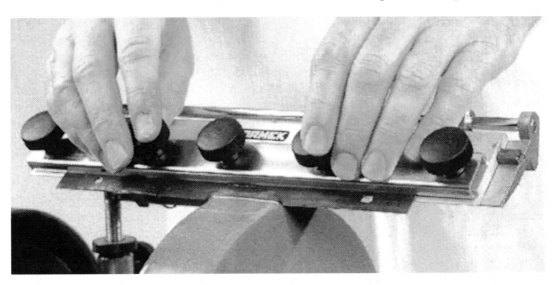

Fig. 176 Attachment to help grind long cutters. (BriMarc Associates)

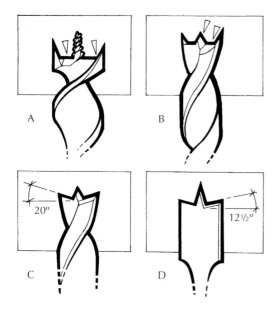

Fig. 177 Sharpening different drill bits: a: auger; b: spur; c: dowel; d: flat.

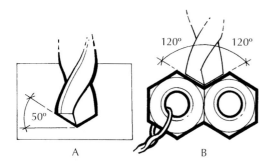

Fig. 178a The correct angle for the end of an engineer's drill bit; and b: a simple home-made guide.

recommended cutting angle is 59 degrees (Fig. 178a), and this can easily be reproduced. As you grind the end, turn it away from the wheel to provide some clearance. If you wish to play around with the cutting angle, then do so. A sharper point will help to pull the drill bit through more quickly, though big bits will take some controlling! A shallower angle will slow the process down. A simple jig that will be close enough to the original angles can be made from a couple of big nuts (Fig. 178b): use large ones and glue or weld them together; it won't matter if they are a degree or so out. There are a few automatic grinders around that are capable of sorting out your engineer's bit all at once. How good they are I am not sure, besides which the job is so simple I feel they can be of no great advantage.

SHARPENING AND SETTING SAWS

So you've decided not to buy those hardpoint saws and have gone for traditional ones instead? Maybe you have some 'oldies' you must do up – well, good luck! With practice and application you will soon master the technique. The worst you can do is to sharpen the saw so that it ends up with a hollowed cutting edge, or set it to run off to one side. The key to sharpening saws is to have the right tools for the job and to take your time. I will only describe the basics here, because they will apply to whatever saw you are sharpening. As you become more proficient you might like to experiment a bit – for instance, depending upon the materials being cut and the quality of finish, you might reduce or increase the set. Certainly for ripsawing it would be silly to have too fine a set: you're bound to bind up eventually! Tenon and dovetail

edges easier to sharpen. **Flat bits** are reasonably simple to do on a grinder provided you maintain the original angles (Fig.177d). Remember to provide some clearance to the side cutting edges to ensure they don't burn during use.

Engineer's bits are always breaking, especially the small ones: if the break leaves them too short, throw them away; if they are long enough, regrind them. The

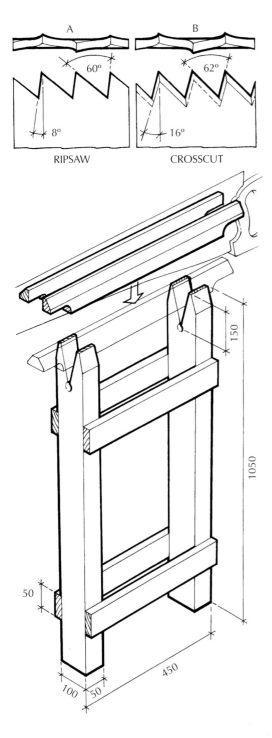

Fig. 179 Sharp saws: a: ripsaw teeth; b: crosscut teeth; c: a set of saw 'chops'.

saws can be very effective with little set, and are more accurate to use. With new saws it is reasonably easy to follow the manufacturer's angles when touching up, and really the procedure should be standard (Fig. 179a and b). If the whole thing needs redoing it becomes more difficult, and such a task cannot be fully covered here.

First, go along to your hardware store and buy the appropriate tapered file for the job. Now make up a set of saw 'chops' (Fig. 179c): these will hold the blade firmly whilst you work on it. Make sure there is enough room below the two loose pieces to take a back saw. For sharpening, the teeth should protrude about 12mm or so and be fully supported throughout the length being worked on. Before starting to sharpen the saw it may need 'topping out', a process that levels off the tips of the teeth to ensure you have a straight row when finished. The process can be carried out in the chops. If you are confident enough, simply run a mill file, lengthways, down across the tips of the teeth until they are straight. This should not take a great deal of effort, particularly as you should never take off more than you need to. You can make a simple jig to hold the file if you want to; it can often be better than doing it freehand (Fig. 180a). Lastly you will need a sawset, the gadget that bends the teeth out from the saw blade to create the kerf. A variety of these are available on the market; one of the best has a magnifying glass to help you see what you are doing!

Now you are ready to start. There is currently some debate about the sharpening and setting process and which should be done first. Personally, I start by sharpening the saw. Fit the saw into the chops and make sure it is firmly held. If the jaws are not long enough to do the whole blade in one go, just do a bit at a time. Depending upon the blade being sharpened, stand easy and in a comfortable position for right-angle or angled filing (Fig. 180b and c).

Every other tooth should be sharpened from the inside to the outside with two or three strokes of the file; you'll soon get into a rhythm. Don't stretch, or move your body or the chops. Mark with a bit of chalk the last tooth sharpened so that you don't lose your place. When you have done all the teeth on one side, turn the whole thing round and do the other side; this will complete the sharpening process.

Now to set the saw. Most setting mechanisms relate to the number of tpi: more for less and less for more. Your tool should identify the number of teeth and the position to set it at. The actual setting process can be carried out in the chops or on the bench. Select alternate teeth and apply the setter; it will push the tooth out a predetermined amount. Make sure you exert the same amount of pressure each time; if the handles are supposed to be closed, then close them. Swap round and do the other side. Don't forget to mark where you got to with chalk; this saves having to do some of the teeth again. Clean off the blade and the bench, put the kit away – and the job is done. Now go and give the saw a try. A couple more sessions and you'll be an expert!

SHARPENING CHISELS AND PLANE IRONS

The basic principle is the same for both these cutting tools, so I will deal with them together. Depending upon how blunt the blades are, there will be one or two processes to follow. Let's assume that they're very blunt! The first thing to do is to regrind them on a dry or wet grinder at about 25 degrees; it is most important at this stage, for general purpose use, to get a straight edge. Be careful not to overheat

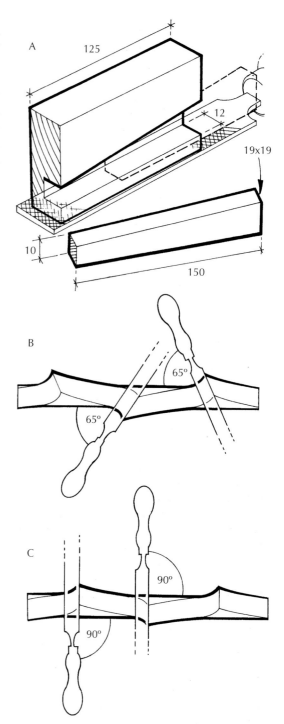

Fig. 180a A 'topping out' device; b: sharpening crosscut teeth; c: sharpening ripsaw teeth.

the cutting edge when grinding – keep it cool by dipping it in water. When you are about right you will notice 'spark out' along the top edge: this is when the grinding stone is in full contact with the surface it is working on, and small sparks fly away from the top edge. It is at this point that it is most likely to overheat, so take care. With chisels I generally mark a pencil line on the back to give me a guideline to work to on the tool rest. If you are not confident about this process, then consider buying a special guide attachment for your grinder. They certainly help with the wider blades.

Honing starts on a coarse gritstone, unless you're just touching up an edge, and the honed angle should be about 30 degrees, though you may wish to experiment with this. Assuming you are going to hone at the standard angle, the aim is to create a small flat at the very tip of the ground edge. Lubricate the stone well, and be sure you keep doing this regularly throughout the process. Place the ground blade face down to the stone, and make contact right across it; you can tell if you have by slightly lifting the back end and letting it go – with your fingers positioned at the front, it should rock back into place. To get the 30 degrees, lift the back of the blade or the top of the handle slightly; in effect this lifts the blade so that it rides on the front leading edge and will be close enough for most jobs. Now run the blade alternately back and forth and in a figure eight (Fig. 181a); this action will help to maintain a flat surface on the oilstone, and to hone the edge evenly. Check the edge often: it should not take many circuits to create the small flat, and the fewer you make, the better. Turn the blade over and, holding it flat against the oilstone surface, rub in a circular motion to remove the burr (Fig. 181b); always finish with a stroke away from you. Repeat the process on a finer gritstone to finish

off. If a tiny burr remains, gently draw the cutting edge through a piece of gash wood to remove it.

Practice will make perfect, and once you have gone through all your edge tools and sharpened them up, nothing is worse than picking up a chisel to find it's blunt! The grinding bit of the process will probably only have to be repeated every third or fourth time. Re-honing will return an edge until the flat gets too wide. If you're not confident about maintaining the honing angle, then buy a jig. There are several on the market, and one that provides adjustable angles is best (Fig. 181c). You can, of course, make you own (Fig. 181d), a cheap and cheerful way to get the angles right.

SHARPENING AND CARING FOR ROUTER CUTTERS

If you knock chunks out of your cutters then there is little that can be done for them. Getting them reground professionally may be an option but will probably not be cost effective; a new one in most cases will be cheaper. Because they are reasonably expensive it's always best to look after them in the first instance.

For cleaning you'll need a solvent to get rid of any resin build-up. If that doesn't work, an abrasive cleaner may have to be used. If the cutter has a guide roller, take it off. Soak all in solvent overnight if you have time. Using a stiff bristle brush, clean all the dirt off. If you can't shift it, try the abrasive cleaner with, dare I say it, one of those little brass suede brushes! But watch the cutting edges. Rinse everything off and wipe with a dry cloth.

Honing all the cutting edges may not be possible; you can really only do the flat

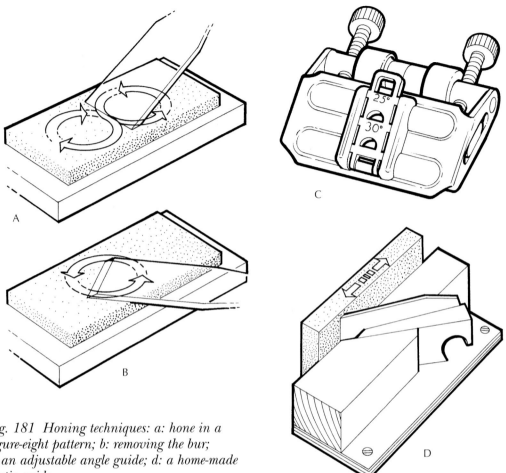

Fig. 181 Honing techniques: a: hone in a figure-eight pattern; b: removing the bur; c: an adjustable angle guide; d: a home-made static guide.

ones. You'll need a range of the small diamond stones for this part: choose a fine grit. Holding the cutter firmly on the bench, position yourself in such a way that you can stroke the flat underface with the stone. You will find it useful to protect the cutter from damage by resting it on stiff foam or something similar. Remember that the cutter is balanced and probably has two cutting edges; to maintain the balance and not damage your router bearings, count the strokes for the first side and then repeat them on the second. Two or three strokes will be enough in

most cases, but always check the edge to see how you're doing. One of my colleagues uses a magnifying glass for this. When you have finished, make sure the cutter is clean and bright. Store it in a box away from moisture to avoid rust. I find it best to keep one of those moisture-absorbing sachets in the box with the cutters; alternatively, coat with a thin oil or silicone spray.

Look after your cutters, and they will give you hours of life in return; they are much too expensive to throw away just because they're blunt!

— 9 —

HEALTHY, WEALTHY AND WISE

Throughout this book, at appropriate points in the text, I have emphasized the need for safety. Here I shall recap, and also examine one of the most critical aspects, dust control. To augment this latter issue we have been fortunate enough to receive permission from the Health and Safety Executive to reproduce some of their information sheets on the subject. Because space is at a premium within this book, we have only been able to publish extracts from sheets numbers 1 and 14; these are found at the end of the chapter. I would urge you to contact your local H&SE offices and ask for a full set of woodworking fact sheets. They are free of charge and contain invaluable information for the woodworker.

Is using basic hand tools dangerous? Well, anything that's sharp can cut, and it isn't always the wood you intended to use the tool on. Even the simple job of starting off a handsaw can lead to a cut thumb – I know: I have done it too often. One of the worst scenarios is when you've nearly finished a job on some light wood and you nick your finger – you don't want blood all over the face of your work, but the plasters are in the house.... What do you do, suck it or wrap an old rag around it? So here's the first bit of advice: keep a fully stocked first aid box in the workshop, and write on a sticky label the telephone numbers of the local surgery, and the general and eye hospitals. Stick this on the outside of the

box where you can see it in an emergency. Here are a few more common sense pointers:

* Powered hand tools are designed to cut automatically, of course; and if you stick any part of your anatomy near the sharp or moving bits, you'll come off worse.

* Wear safety glasses, and keep long hair and loose clothing tied back.

* Make sure the workpiece is securely fixed before you start.

* Don't let yourself be startled by someone disturbing you.

* Use 110-volt equipment, or fit circuit breakers to all power points.

* Never tamper with the guards: if you remove them to fit a cutter, then put them

Fig. 182 Keep the workshop clean with a vacuum. (Record Power Tools)

about and attach to tools (Fig. 183). When you buy powered tools, check to see that they have a dust or shavings outlet port, and examine your fittings to make sure you can connect them (Fig. 184).

Fig. 183 A mobile vacuum hooked up to a power tool. (Record Power Tools)

Fig. 184 All sanders, especially belt sanders, should be hooked into an extraction system. (Record Power Tools)

back on afterwards: they're there for a reason.

* Make sure the tool has stopped before you put it down, and fully disconnect it so that it can't be switched on inadvertently.

* Don't leave rubbish and off-cuts lying around on the bench or floor.

* Ban all children unless under direct supervision.

Remember that a tidy workshop produces tidy work. I can't bear it when the workshop's in a mess. I know I've got to put up with it; sometimes during the manufacturing process there is bound to be a mess – probably I clean up too often. But leaving bits and pieces lying around on the floor is asking for trouble, and dust and shavings on the bench will get mixed up with everything else – so clear it up (Fig. 182). A portable vacuum is a good investment: make sure it is easy to carry

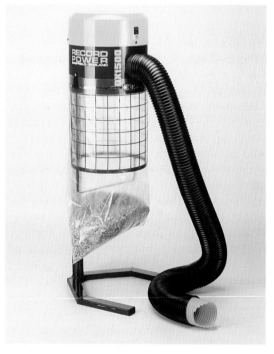

Fig. 185 A free-standing vacuum extraction system. (Record Power Tools)

Fig. 186 A portable air filter that can be hung anywhere the lead will let it. (Microlene UK Limited)

Bigger chip and dust extractors are available (Fig. 185): read the literature carefully, or ask questions before you buy. The most important thing to look out for, apart from the size of motor and its suck rate, is the 'dust' extraction capability of the machine. They will all suck in air, dust, sawdust and chippings – what you need to look at is how the exhaust air is filtered, and where it goes to. This is the crucial health and safety issue: how much residual dust is exhausted from the machine? Fabric filters, through which the exhaust air is blown, will not be as efficient as paper ones; perhaps the best rule of thumb is, the more filters there are, the better! You'll soon know how successful your machine is at removing dust once it's

installed. At the end of the day put a polished, clean surface on the bench and check for dust next morning; you'll probably be surprised. If possible it's a good idea to position the extractor unit outside or in another building; then the exhausted air will go elsewhere.

If you already have a unit, or have decided on the simple type of extractor, then there are some other options to consider; for instance, you could install air filters that can be positioned in strategic places, over and around the bench – it's the dust you can't see that will have the most harmful effect on your health. Small filters are reasonably priced and can be hung immediately over the workstation (Fig. 186); with enough cable you can move these around and they are very

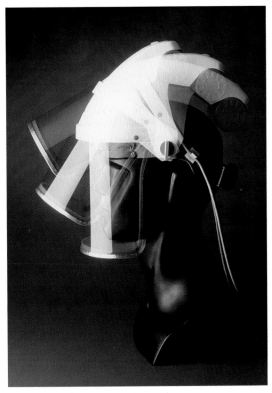

Fig. 187 A full-face battery-powered respirator. (Record Power Tools)

Fig. 188 A more substantial, static air filter. (Microlene UK Limited)

effective, as long as there's somewhere to hang them from. If you have a big space to deal with, then larger, more commercial units are available (Fig. 188) – although unless you can build a portable frame these are static and should, therefore, be positioned carefully. Ambient air filters will help remove the very fine dust that can damage your health.

The second option is to go for a full-face powered respirator (Fig. 187); this is a wonderful bit of kit that really works, provided you clean the filters regularly. They are quite hot to use in summer, but air does circulate to help keep you cool.

In my workshop I have installed a small industrial vacuum extraction unit, and I use a full-face respirator; for me this is the best combination. I would advise that at the very least you wear a nose and mouth facemask; they are not as efficient, but they will take some of the fine dust out of the air you breathe before it gets into your lungs. Read on now and take note of what the Health and Safety Executive has to say on the subject. Their words may do more than mine to convince you to work in a safe, clean and tidy workshop!

EXTRACTS FROM HEALTH & SAFETY EXECUTIVE WOODWORKING SHEETS 1 & 14

WOODWORKING SHEET NO 1: WOOD DUST: HAZARDS AND PRECAUTIONS

The main operations likely to produce high dust levels in the woodworking industry are:

1 machining operations, particularly sawing, routing and turning;
2 sanding, by machine and by hand; and
3 using compressed air lines to blow dust off furniture and other articles before spraying.

High airborne dust levels can also occur during factory cleaning, especially when compressed air lines are used for blowing dust from walls, ledges and other surfaces.

What are the hazards?

Health
Too much dust of any kind can adversely affect health. Wood dust is no exception. Exposure has been associated with the following health problems:

1 skin disorders;
2 obstruction in the nose;
3 a type of asthma; and
4 a rare type of nasal cancer

The Control of Substances Hazardous to Health Regulations 1988 (COSHH)3.4 came into force on 1 October 1989 and, by virtue of Regulation 6(1), an assessment (normally written) should be made of risks to health associated with wood dust, together with any action needed to prevent or control those risks.

Regulation 7(1) goes on to say that exposure to both hardwood and softwood dust should be prevented, or where this is not reasonably practicable, adequately controlled.

Hardwood dust has been assigned a maximum exposure limit (MEL) of 5mg/m3 (8-hour time weighted average) in Schedule 1 of the Regulations and therefore exposure by inhalation to hardwood dust should be reduced so far as is reasonably practicable and, in any case. Below the MEL. Detailed guidance on the health effects of hardwood dust and the precautions required are given in HSE leaflet *Hardwood Dust.*

Sollwood dust has not been allocated an occupational exposure limit under the COSHH Regulations but the HSC's Advisory Committee on Toxic Substances intends to review exposure to the substance. However, pending the outcome of this review, the limit of 5mg/m3 (8-hour HSE Guidance Note EH40 *Occupational Exposure Limits*, should be used as guidance for the control of exposure under Regulation 7(1).

Fire/explosion
Each year premises and plant are severely damaged or destroyed by wood dust fires and explosions. Concentrations of small dust particles in the air can form a mixture that will explode if ignited. These concentrations usually occur in dust extraction equipment which can be destroyed unless special precautions are taken. Such an explosion can also dislodge dust deposits that may have accumulated on walls, floors and ledges which in turn can ignite causing a secondary explosion.

Wood dust will also burn readily if ignited. Fires can be started by badly maintained heating units, overheated electric motors, electric sparks and sparks from other sources such as open wood burning stoves and cigarettes.

Safety
Wood dust on the floor can cause tripping or slipping. Vision can be impaired by airborne chips and dust generated during machining and sanding operations.

WOODWORKING SHEET NO 14: SELECTION OF RESPIRATORY PROTECTIVE EQUIPMENT SUITABLE FOR USE WITH WOOD DUST

Introduction
This information sheet is one of a series prepared by HSE's Woodworking National Interest Group. Its purpose is to advise employers on the selection of respiratory protective equipment (RPE) for use with wood dust, both hardwood and softwood. All wood dust (including dust from composites like chipboards and fibre boards etc) is hazardous to health: it can affect the nose, the respiratory system and the skin.

Dust respirators will give no protection at all against gases and vapours (e.g. from paint spraying).

The Control of Substances Hazardous to Health (COSHH) Regulations 1994 require employers to assess the risks and precautions needed to prevent or control exposure to hazardous substances such as wood dust. The first priority should always be to prevent exposure or, if this is not possible, to control it at source, for example by effective local exhaust ventilation.

RPE is no substitute for effective control of dust at source.

Personal protection (such as protective clothing and respirators) may be needed as an interim measure where engineering controls are being developed and/or modified and for short-term jobs such as cleaning and maintenance. Engineering controls protect everyone in the workplace; personal protective equipment can only help the person who wears it.

Dust respirators filter the air breathed by the wearer in order to make it safe to breathe and are not suitable for use in situations where the amount of oxygen in the air may be deficient, e.g. in confined spaces. These situations require breathing apparatus which provides air from an independent source (e.g. a cylinder).

Selection
RPE used to protect against wood dust must meet two basic requirements:

1 The RPE must be suitable for the purpose for which it is used. This means that it must provide effective protection to the wearer in the circumstances in which it is worn. It must be capable of providing a sufficient quality of clean air for the wearer to breathe. It must fit the wearer and the wearer must use it properly in accordance with the manufacturer's instructions. If the respirator is not a disposable 'one shift' type, it must also be cleaned daily and maintained in accordance with the manufacturer's instructions.

2 RPE must be CE marked. You may have some equipment manufactured before 1 July 1995 that is not CE marked – it should have Health and Safety Executive approval (see reference 4). Such equipment can continue to be used as long as it is suitable (see paragraph 1 above) and well maintained.

Table 1 is designed to help those in woodworking to select suitable respirators. Only the most common types used in woodworking are included, ie the disposable respirator, the half- and full-mask dust respirators and lightweight powered visors and helmets. This does not mean that other types are not suitable, and guidance on their selection can be found in *Respiratory protective equipment: A practical guide for users.*

There are some simple masks, known as nuisance dust masks, which do not give any reliable protection against substances hazardous to health. These should not be used with wood dust.

Personal and work-related factors in selection of RPE
All types of RPE restrict the wearer to some extent, by imposing extra breathing resistance on the lungs and by restricting visibility or mobility. These restrictions underline the need to control exposures by other means wherever possible. It is also important to remember that effective protection is only given when equipment which is of the right standard and in good condition is properly fitted and used. Removal of the RPE, even for short periods, dramatically reduces the level of protection afforded to the wearer.

A respirator which is not worn or is hung around the neck gives no protection at all.

Face masks depend on good contact between the skin and the mask for their effectiveness. Many face masks are available in one size only and cannot be expected to fit all the working population. A good fit and seal are essential – without them the respirator will not give effective protection. It is advisable to obtain a selection of different models of RPE so that masks can be selected to give the best fit for individual wearers. It will only be possible to get a good seal if the skin in the region of the seal is smooth and without hair. Facial hair or glasses will tend to lift the mask off the face and permit inward leakage of contaminated air. A simple check on how well a face mask fits can be done in the following way:

1 Put on the equipment according to the manufacturer's instructions.
2 For disposable respirators, cup the hands over the whole of the facepiece; for respirators with separate filters, cover the inlet to the filter with the hands or with a flat sheet of card or similar material.
3 Inhale sharply so that the mask collapses slightly. Hold the breath.
4 If the mask remains collapsed for a few seconds and no leakage is detected, the mask probably fits adequately.
5 If leakage is detected, the headstraps should be re-adjusted and the test repeated. If leakage persists a different size or design of respirator is needed.

Crown copyright material is reproduced with the permission of the Controller of Her Majesty's Stationery Office.

GLOSSARY

arris The sharp point at which, say, a top and side meet.

badger A large rebate plane.

ball off To cut away quickly a large amount of waste with a plane.

bandings Narrow, patterned inlays.

bare Slightly under size.

bead A small round moulding.

Birmingham screwdriver Driving a screw in using a hammer.

body The main part of any tool.

carborundum Carbide of silicon.

chamfer To cut away a sharp edge with a prominent bevel equal on both sides.

chops A device made to hold the blade of a saw ridged during the sharpening process.

chuck A two-, three- or four-jaw device for holding, generally, drill bits.

cpm Cuts per minute.

dig in When a tool has been misguided and dug into the wrong part of a surface.

dog An adjustable stop.

dovetail This is a strong and versatile joint that, when some components are cut, looks similar to the fantail of a dove.

dressed Timber that is planed on one or more sides.

edge The narrow surfaces of wooden rectangular sections.

face The wide surfaces of wooden rectangular sections. Also the face or finished side, the best surface.

full Slightly oversize.

ground The base onto which a veneer is fixed.

gullet The space between two consecutive saw teeth.

haft The handle or shaft of a striking tool.

half crowns Damage to the surface caused by miss-hitting with a hammer.

hand A term used to denote which side something is fixed to, or is a part of.

housing A trench or groove in one piece of wood into which another fits.

HSS High speed steel, hardened steel.

inlay Small, decorative strips of wood cut into a surface to enhance it.

jig A pattern or template that can also hold the workpiece.

keep A grooved strip of plastic or wood that protects saw teeth.

lumber A term used to describe sawn timbers.

M2 This indicates how many square metres there are when prefixed with the appropriate number.

M3 This indicates how many cubic metres there are when prefixed with the appropriate number.

M4, M6, M8 etc This is a common marking found on bolts and threaded bars. Its combined indication tells us that the thread is metric and what the diameter is in mm.

MC Moisture content.

MDF Medium density fiberboard.

mitre The joining point of two pieces forming an angle, not necessarily 45 degrees.

mm This indicates how many millimetres there are when prefixed with the appropriate number.

mouldings Long lengths of wood shaped to specific patterns, squares or rectangles.

par Planed all round.

ppi Points per inch on a saw blade.

pse Planed and square-edged.

ptg Planed, tongued and grooved.

rpm Revolutions per minute.

spelshing The furry, spiky bits that protrude from the underside of a saw cut.

std Standard.

sts Sawn to size.

tang The part of a tool, say chisel, that fits up inside the handle.

tct Tungsten carbide tip, a very hard inserted tooth or edge.

TG & V Tongued, grooved and V-jointed.

tpi Teeth per inch on a saw blade.

universal woodworker A machine capable of a number of different tasks, say, planing, sawing and boring etc.

veneer A thin layer of wood glued onto another, thicker piece called a ground.

WD40 A freely available, thin lubricating and penetrating oil.

INDEX